A Text Book Of

PROCEDURE ORIENTED PROGRAMMING USING C

For
For Semester - V : B.B.A. (Computer Application)
Formerly known as B.C.A.

As Per Revised Syllabus
Effective from June 2013

Rajesh S. Yemul
B.E. (Comp.), MISTE
Lecturer in Computer Department
Sou. Venutai Chavan Polytechnic
Vadgaon (Bk)
Pune

N2931

Procedure Oriented Programming Using C ISBN 978-93-83525-96-6

Third Edition : January 2016
© : Author

The text of this publication, or any part thereof, should not be reproduced or transmitted in any form or stored in any computer storage system or device for distribution including photocopy, recording, taping or information retrieval system or reproduced on any disc, tape, perforated media or other information storage device etc., without the written permission of Author with whom the rights are reserved. Breach of this condition is liable for legal action.

Every effort has been made to avoid errors or omissions in this publication. In spite of this, errors may have crept in. Any mistake, error or discrepancy so noted and shall be brought to our notice shall be taken care of in the next edition. It is notified that neither the publisher nor the author or seller shall be responsible for any damage or loss of action to any one, of any kind, in any manner, therefrom.

Published By :
NIRALI PRAKASHAN
Abhyudaya Pragati, 1312, Shivaji Nagar
Off J.M. Road, PUNE – 411005
Tel - (020) 25512336/37/39, Fax - (020) 25511379
Email : niralipune@pragationline.com

Printed By :
Repro Knowledgecast Limited,
Thane

☐ DISTRIBUTION CENTRES

PUNE
Nirali Prakashan : 119, Budhwar Peth, Jogeshwari Mandir Lane, Pune 411002, Maharashtra
Tel : (020) 2445 2044, 66022708, Fax : (020) 2445 1538
Email : bookorder@pragationline.com, niralilocal@pragationline.com

Nirali Prakashan : S. No. 28/27, Dhyari, Near Pari Company, Pune 411041
Tel : (020) 24690204 Fax : (020) 24690316
Email : dhyari@pragationline.com, bookorder@pragationline.com

MUMBAI
Nirali Prakashan : 385, S.V.P. Road, Rasdhara Co-op. Hsg. Society Ltd.,
Girgaum, Mumbai 400004, Maharashtra
Tel : (022) 2385 6339 / 2386 9976, Fax : (022) 2386 9976
Email : niralimumbai@pragationline.com

☐ DISTRIBUTION BRANCHES

JALGAON
Nirali Prakashan : 34, V. V. Golani Market, Navi Peth, Jalgaon 425001,
Maharashtra, Tel : (0257) 222 0395, Mob : 94234 91860

KOLHAPUR
Nirali Prakashan : New Mahadvar Road, Kedar Plaza, 1st Floor Opp. IDBI Bank
Kolhapur 416 012, Maharashtra. Mob : 9850046155

NAGPUR
Pratibha Book Distributors : Above Maratha Mandir, Shop No. 3, First Floor,
Rani Jhanshi Square, Sitabuldi, Nagpur 440012, Maharashtra
Tel : (0712) 254 7129

DELHI
Nirali Prakashan : 4593/21, Basement, Aggarwal Lane 15, Ansari Road, Daryaganj
Near Times of India Building, New Delhi 110002
Mob : 08505972553

BENGALURU
Pragati Book House : House No. 1, Sanjeevappa Lane, Avenue Road Cross,
Opp. Rice Church, Bengaluru – 560002.
Tel : (080) 64513344, 64513355,Mob : 9880582331, 9845021552
Email:bharatsavla@yahoo.com

CHENNAI
Pragati Books : 9/1, Montieth Road, Behind Taas Mahal, Egmore,
Chennai 600008 Tamil Nadu, Tel : (044) 6518 3535,
Mob : 94440 01782 / 98450 21552 / 98805 82331,
Email : bharatsavla@yahoo.com

niralipune@pragationline.com | www.pragationline.com
Also find us on www.facebook.com/niralibooks

Preface ...

I take this opportunity to present this book entitled as **"Procedure Oriented Programming Using C"** to the students of Second Semester [BBA (Computer Application)]. The object of this book is to present the subject matter in a most concise and simple manner. The book is written strictly according to the Revised Syllabus.

The book has its own unique features. It brings out the subject in a very simple and lucid manner for easy and comprehensive understanding of the basic concepts, its intricacies, procedures and practices. This book will help the readers to have a broader view on Procedure Oriented Programming Using C. The language used in this book is easy and will help students to improve their vocabulary of Technical terms and understand the matter in a better and happier way.

I sincerely thank Shri. Dineshbhai Furia and Shri. Jignesh Furia of Nirali Prakashan for the confidence reposed in me and giving me this opportunity to reach out to the students of management studies.

I thank Prof. Gautam Bapat for the friendly manner in which he reviewed our script and suggested improvements from time to time, i must say he has done the editing, exceptionally well for our book.

I thank Mr. Amar Salunkhe for his important inputs time to time and Mr. Akbar Shaikh who painstakingly attended to all the details to make this book appear good.

I also thank Ms. Chaitali Takale, Mr. Ravindra Walodare, Mr. Mahesh Swami, Mr. Vijay Shete, Mr. Sachin Shinde, Nikunj Joshi, Nilesh Deshmukh, Ashok Bodke, Moshin Sayyed and Nitin Thorat.

I have given my best inputs for this book. Any suggestions towards the improvement of this book and sincere comments are most welcome on niralipune@pragationline.com.

AUTHOR

Syllabus ...

1. Introduction to C Language   **[4 Lectures]**
  - 1.1 History
  - 1.2 Basic structure of C Programming
  - 1.3 Language fundamentals
    - 1.3.1 Character set, tokens
    - 1.3.2 Keywords and identifiers
    - 1.3.3 Variables and data types
  - 1.4 Operators
    - 1.4.1 Types of operators
    - 1.4.2 Precedence and associativity
    - 1.4.3 Expression

2. Managing I/O Operations   **[2 Lectures]**
  - 2.1 Console based I/O and related built-in I/O functions
    - 2.1.1 printf(), scanf()
    - 2.1.2 getch(), getchar()
  - 2.2 Formatted input and formatted output

3. Decision Making and Looping   **[6 Lectures]**
  - 3.1 Introduction
  - 3.2 Decision Making Structure
    - 3.2.1 If statement
    - 3.2.2 If-else statement
    - 3.2.3 Nested if-else statement
    - 3.2.4 Conditional operator
    - 3.2.5 Switch statement
  - 3.3 Loop Control Structures
    - 3.3.1 while loop
    - 3.3.2 Do-while loop
    - 3.3.3 For loop
    - 3.3.4 Nested for loop
  - 3.4 Jump statements
    - 3.4.1 break
    - 3.4.2 continue
    - 3.4.3 goto
    - 3.4.4 exit

4. Functions and Pointers   **[12 Lectures]**
  - 4.1 Introduction
    - 4.1.1 Purpose of function
    - 4.1.2 Function definition
    - 4.1.3 Function declaration
    - 4.1.4 Function call
  - 4.2 Types of functions
  - 4.3 Call by value and call by reference
  - 4.4 Storage classes
  - 4.5 Recursion

4.6 Introduction to pointer
    4.6.1 Definition
    4.6 2 Declaration
    4.6.3 Initialization
4.7 Indirection operator and address of operator
4.8 Pointer arithmetic
4.9 Dynamic memory allocation
4.10 Functions and pointers

5. Arrays and Strings [8 Lectures]
5.1 Introduction to one-dimensional Array
    5.1.1 Definition
    5.1.2 Declaration
    5.1.3 Initialization
5.2 Accessing and displaying array elements
5.3 Arrays and functions
5.4 Introduction to two-dimensional Array
    5.4.1 Definition
    5.4.2 Declaration
    5.4.3 Initialization
5.5 Accessing and displaying array elements
5.6 Introductions to Strings
    5.6.1 Definition
    5.6.2 Declaration
    5.6.3 Initialization
5.7 Standard library functions
5.8 Implementations without standard library functions.

6. Structures and Union [5 Lectures]
6.1 Introduction to structure
    6.1.1 Definition
    6.1.2 Declaration
    6.1.3 Accessing members
6.2 Structure Operations
6.3 Nested Structure
6.4 Introduction to union
    6.4.1 Definition
    6.4.2 Declaration
6.5 Differentiate between Structure and Union

7. C Preprocessor [2 Lectures]
7.1 Definition of preprocessor
7.2 Macro substitution directory
7.3 File inclusion directory
7.4 Conditional compilation

8. File Handling [9 Lectures]
8.1 Definitions of files
8.2 File opening modes
8.3 Standard functions
8.4 Random access to files
8.5 Command line argument

●●●

Contents ...

1. **Introduction to C Language**   1.1 – 1.32

2. **Managing I/O Operations**   2.1 – 2.10

3. **Decision Making and Looping**   3.1 – 3.56

4. **Functions and Pointers**   4.1 – 4.56

5. **Arrays and Strings**   5.1 – 5.64

6. **Structures and Union**   6.1 – 6.20

7. **C Preprocessor**   7.1 – 7.10

8. **File Handling**   8.1 – 8.26

Question Papers : October 2014, April 2015, November 2015   P.1 – P.9

●●●

Chapter 1...

Introduction to C Language

Contents ...

1.1 Introduction to C Language
    1.1.1 Features of C
    1.1.2 Advantages
    1.1.3 Disadvantages
1.2 History of C
1.3 Basic Structure of C Programming
1.4 C Language Fundamentals
    1.4.1 Character Set
    1.4.2 Tokens
    1.4.3 Keywords
    1.4.4 Identifiers
    1.4.5 Constants
    1.4.6 Variables
        1.4.6.1 Declaring and Initializing Variables
        1.4.6.2 Types of Variables
    1.4.7 Data Types
1.5 Operators
    1.5.1 Types of Operators
    1.5.2 Precedence and Associativity of Operators
    1.5.3 Expressions
- Questions

1.1 Introduction to C Language

- C language is a general purpose and structured programming language developed by 'Dennis Ritchie' at AT&T's Bell Laboratories in the 1972s in USA.

Dennis Ritchie
(1.1)

- A structured programming language offers a variety of programming possibilities and capabilities. It support different control loops, different statements etc.
- C language combines the best elements of high-level language with control and flexibility of assembly language so it is a middle level language.
- C language is also called as 'Procedure oriented programming language.'
- C is a Middle level languages that don't provide all the built-in functions found in high level languages, but provides all building blocks that we need to produce the result we want.
- C language allows the programmer to write low level programs as well as high level programs so it is called as middle level language.
- C has now become a widely used professional language for following reasons:
    1. C language is easy to learn.
    2. C language is structured language.
    3. C language produces efficient programs.
    4. C language can handle low-level activities.
    5. C language can be compiled on a variety of computers.

1.1.1 Features of C

- C language consist of following features:
    1. **Middle Level Language:** C is a middle level language as it combines elements of high-level language with the functional of assembly language. C allows direct manipulation of bits, bytes, words, and pointers.
    2. **Block Structured Language:** C is referred as a structured language because it is similar in many ways to other structured languages like ALGOL, Pascal and the likes. C allows compartmentalization of code and data. This is a distinguishing feature of any structured language.
    3. **Code Portability:** The code written in C is machine independent which means, there is no change in 'C' instructions, when you change the Operating System or Hardware. There is hardly any change required to compile when you move the program from one environment to another.
    4. **Recursion:** A function may call itself again and again this feature is called as recursion, is supported by C.
    5. **Efficiency:** C provides fast program execution.
    6. **High level language feature:** This feature allows the programmer to concentrate on the logic flow of the code.

7. **Low level features:** C has a close relationship with assembly languages. So it is easy to make assembly program in C.
8. **Powerful:** C is very powerful language since low level commands have been access like assembly language.
9. **Flexibility:** In C language programmer has many ways to accomplish the same task.
10. **Small size:** C language provides no input output facilities. This helps to keep program small.
11. One important feature of C program, is its ability to extend itself.

1.1.2 Advantages

- Various advantages of C language are:
    1. C is a building block for many other currently know languages.
    2. It is Portable Programming Language. This means a program written for one computer may run successfully on other computer also.
    3. It is fast for executing. This means that the executable program obtained after compiling and linking runs very fast.
    4. It is compact Programming Language. The statements in C Language are generally short but very powerful.
    5. It is simple/easy. The C Language has both the simplicity of High Level Language and the speed of Low Level Language. So it is also know as Middle Level Language.
    6. It has only 32 keyword so that are easy to remember.
    7. Its compiler is easily available.
    8. It has ability to extend itself. Users can add their own functions to the C Library.
    9. It can use to design middle type of software.

1.1.3 Disadvantages

- Various disadvantages of C language are:
    1. There is no run-time checking.
    2. There is no strict type checking, (for example: We can pass an integer value for floating data type).
    3. As the program extends it is very difficult to fix the bugs.
    4. It may be compile time overhead due to the misplacing and excessive use of pointers.
    5. It does not use to develop complex type of software now a day.

1.2 History of C

- The development of C was a cause of evolution of programming languages like ALGOL 60, CPL (Combined Programming Language), BCPL (Basic Combined Programming Language) and B.
- Fig. 1.1 shows brief history of C language.
- C was developed by Dennis Ritchie at Bell Laboratories in 1972. Most of its principles and ideas were taken from the earlier language B, BCPL and CPL.
- CPL was developed jointly between the Mathematical Laboratory at the University of Cambridge and the University of London Computer Unit in 1960s.
- CPL (Combined Programming Language) was developed with the purpose of creating a language that was capable of both machine independent programming and would allow the programmer to control the behavior of individual bits of information. But the CPL was too large for use in many applications.
- In 1967, BCPL (Basic Combined Programming Language) was created as a scaled down version of CPL while still retaining its basic features. This process was continued by Ken Thompson. He made B Language during working at Bell Labs.
- B Language was a scaled down version of BCPL. B Language was written for the systems programming.
- In 1972, a co-worker of Ken Thompson, Dennis Ritchie developed C Language by taking some of the generality found in BCPL to the B language.
- The original PDP-11 version of the Unix system was developed in assembly language.
- In 1973, C language had become powerful enough that most of the Unix kernel was rewritten in C. This was one of the first operating system kernels implemented in a language other than assembly.
- In 1978, Dennis Ritchie and Brian Kernighan published the first edition "The C Programming Language" and commonly known as K&R C
- The 1989 standard for C is commonly referred as C89.
- During 1990s the development of C++ language consumed most programmers attention but work on C continued quietly along with a new standard for C being developed and the result was the 1999 standard for C, usually referred as C99. It retained all features of C89.

Year of establishment	Language name	Description
1960	ALGOL-60 ⇓	ALGOL is an acronym for Algorithmic Language developed by Cambridge University. It was the first structured procedural programming language, developed in the late 1950s and once widely used in Europe. But it was too abstract and too general structured language.
1963	CPL (Combined Programming Language) ⇓	CPL is an acronym for Combined Programming Language. It was developed at Cambridge University.
1967	BCPL (Basic Combined Programming Language) ⇓	BCPL is an acronym for Basic Combined Programming Language. It was developed by Martin Richards at Cambridge University in 1967. BCPL was not so powerful. So, it was failed.
1970	B ⇓	B language was developed by Ken Thompson at AT & T Bell Laboratories in 1970. It was machine dependent. So, it leads to specific problems.
1972	C ⇓	'C' Programming Language was developed by Dennis Ritchie at AT & T Bell Laboratories in 1972. This is general purpose, compiled, structured programming language. Dennis Ritchie studied the BCPL, then improved and named it as 'C' which is the second letter of BCPL.
1978	K&R C ⇓	Dennis Ritchie and Brian Kernighan published the first edition "The C Programming Language" and commonly known as K&R C.
1989	C89/C90 standard ⇓	First standardized specification for C language was developed by American National Standards Institute in 1989. C89 and C90 standards refer to the same programming language.
1999	C99 standard	Next revision was published in 1999 that introduced new futures like advanced data types and other changes. It retained nearly all of the features of C89, thus C is still C.

Fig. 1.1: Brief History of C language

1.3 Basic Structure of C Programming

- Following blocks shows structure of a C programming.

```
Library File Access
Definitions
Declarations
```
```
Functions
main( )
{
    Declarations
    Statements
}
```
```
User-defined functions
funct1( )
{
    :
}
funct2( )
{
    :
    :
}
```

- The C program begin executing at main( ). In the above declaration library file are used to give instructions to compiler for linking purpose.
- All constants and global variables declarations is done here. In second box consists of main( ). Local variable declarations and statements define in main( ).
- The last and third part consists of all user defined functions. These functions are called in main( ) function.

A Simple C Program ("Hello World"):

- Every C program must contain main( ) function. Execution of each and every C program starts with main function only.
- Every C program can contain more than one function but each program has to be a main( ) function in order to execute the program.
- C program is also called as **procedure oriented programming language** where importance is given to the procedure i.e. the task to be done which is expressed in the form of functions. So functions works as a building block for the programs.

- The program prints out "Hello World" to the standard output, which is usually a terminal or screen display.
    1. #include<stdio.h>
    2. int main(void)
    3. {
    4. printf("Hello World\n");
    5. return 0;
    6. }

Explanation of 'C' program are given below:

1. #include<stdio.h>

This first line of the program is a preprocessing directive, **#include**. This causes the preprocessor — the first tool to examine source code as it is compiled — to substitute the line with the entire text of the **stdio.h** file. The header file **stdio.h** contains declarations for standard input and output functions such as **printf**.

2. int main(void)

This line indicates that a function named main is being defined. The main function serves a special purpose in C programs. The run-time environment calls the main function to begin program execution. The type specifier int indicates that the return value, the value of evaluating the main function that is returned to its invoker (in this case the run-time environment), is an integer. The keyword void as a parameter list indicates that the main function takes no arguments.

3. {

This opening curly brace indicates the beginning of the definition of the main function.

4. printf("Hello World\n");

This line calls (executes the code for) a function named **printf**, which is declared in the included header **stdio.h** and supplied from a system library. In this call, the printf function is passed (provided with) a single argument, the address of the first character in the string literal "Hello World\n". The semicolon (;) terminates the statement.

5. return 0;

This line terminates the execution of the main function and causes it to return the integer value 0, which is interpreted by the run-time system as an exit code, (indicating successful execution).

6. }

This closing curly brace indicates the end of the code for the main function.

Compile and execute C program:

- Compilation is the process of converting a C program which is user readable code into machine readable code which is 0's and 1's.
- This compilation process is done by a compiler which is an inbuilt program in C.
- As a result of compilation, we get another file called executable file. This is also called as binary file.
- This binary file is executed to get the output of the program based on the logic written into it.

Steps to compile and execute a C program:

Step 1 : Type the above C basic program in a text editor and save as "sample.c".
Step 2 : To compile this program, open the command prompt and goto the directory where you have saved this program and type "cc sample.c" or "gcc sample.c".
Step 3 : If there is no error in above program, executable file will be generated in the name of "a.out".
Step 4 : To run this executable file, type "./a.out" in command prompt.
Step 5 : You will see the output as shown in the above basic program.

1.4 C Language Fundamentals

1.4.1 Character Set

- Character set are the set of alphabets, letters and some special characters that are valid in C language.
- A character refers to the digit, alphabet or special symbol used to data representation.
- The C character set consists of all uppercase characters A to Z, the lowercase characters a to z, the digits 0 to 9, certain special characters and white spaces.
- The special character are listed below:

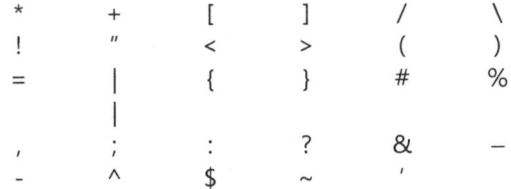

- White space characters:

backspace	\b	Vertical tab	\v
newline	\n	form feed	\f
horizontal tab	\t	carriage return	\r

- These characteristics combinations are known as escape sequence.

1.4.2 Tokens

- In a C program the smallest individual meaningful units is called token.
- C tokens are the basic buildings blocks in C language which are constructed together to write a C program.
- Fig. 1.2 shows various tokens in C language.

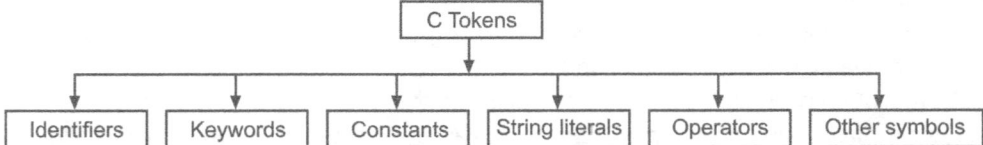

Fig. 1.2: Tokens in C

1. Identifiers are user defined words like sum, roll_no, sub_marks and used for variable and function names.
2. Keywords are reserved words like int, for, while etc.
3. Constants are fixed values which does not change like 10, S etc.
4. Operators are symbols which represents an operation like +, –, * etc.
5. Other symbols are symbols which have particular meaning like ; (semicolon) indicates end of an instruction.
6. String literals is a sequence of zero or more characters enclosed in double quotes like "Nirali Prakashan".

- Fig. 1.3 shows various tokens in C program.

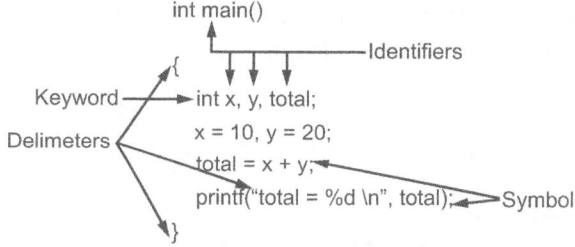

Fig. 1.3: Various token in program

1.4.3 Keywords

- Keywords are the reserved words used in C programming. Each keyword has fixed meaning and that cannot be changed by user.
- Keywords are standard identifiers that have standard predefined meaning in C.
- It is strongly recommended that keywords should be in lower case letters.
- Keywords can be used only for their intended purpose. Keywords can't be used as programmer defined identifier. The keywords can't be used as names for variables.
- There are totally **32 (Thirty Two) keywords** used in a C programming.

int	float	double	long
short	signed	unsigned	const
if	else	switch	break
default	do	while	for
register	extern	static	struct
typedef	enum	return	sizeof
goto	union	auto	case
void	char	continue	volatile

1.4.4 Identifiers
- An identifier is a user define name used to represent program elements such as function names, variables, structures etc.
- Identifier is the name of a variable that is made up from combination of alphabets, digits and underscore.
- Identifiers are created to give unique name to C entities to identify it during the execution of program.
- The rules which should be followed while naming an identifier are:
    1. Identifier name must be a sequence of letter and digits, and must begin with a letter.
    2. The underscore character ('_') is considered as letter.
    3. Names shouldn't be a keyword (such as int , float, if ,break, for etc)
    4. Both upper-case letter and lower-case letter characters are allowed. However, they're not interchangeable.
    5. No identifier may be keyword.
    6. No special characters, such as semicolon,period,blank space, slash or comma are permitted

Examples of valid identifiers:
   sum, sum1, price_of_item, Rate_of_interest, add_odd.

Examples of invalid identifiers:
   2rate, 6a, a + b, x%y
- The length of the identifier can be arbitrarily long but most of the compilers in C recognize only first eight characters.

1.4.5 Constants
- Constants is a fixed value which do not change during program execution.
- Constants are also refer as literals.
- For a particular program we can have certain constants (For example: for calculating area of circle, pi = 3.148 is a constant) so instead of storing them in a particular variable and then using them, we can directly use them.
- Constants can be of any of the basic data type.
- Constants are the terms that can't be changed during the execution of a program. For example: 1, 2.5, "Programming is easy." etc.
- In C, constants can be classified as follows:

1. Integer constants:
- Integer constants are the numeric constants (constant associated with number) without any fractional part or exponential part. There are three types of integer constants in C language decimal constant (base 10), octal constant (base 8) and hexadecimal constant (base 16).
    o Decimal digits: 0 1 2 3 4 5 6 7 8 9.
    o Octal digits: 0 1 2 3 4 5 6 7.
    o Hexadecimal digits: 0 1 2 3 4 5 6 7 8 9 A B C D E F.

For example:
- Decimal constants: 0, -9, 22 etc.
- Octal constants: 021, 077, 033 etc.
- Hexadecimal constants: 0x7f, 0x2a, 0x521 etc

2. **Floating Point Constants:**
- Floating point constants requires the decimal point followed by the number's fractional component.
- We can represent exponential data as constant using floating point constant.
- Floating point constant have following rules:
    (i) They have a decimal point and digits from 0 to 9.
    (ii) Commas and blank spaces are not permitted.
    (iii) They can be negative.
    (iv) It is possible to omit digits before or after the decimal point.

Examples:
(i) 2×10^7 can be present in many ways:
    20000000   2e7   2e 7   2E7   2.0e + 7
    0.2e8   .2E8
(ii) 3.2×10^{-6} can be represent as:
    3.2 E – 6   3.2e – 6 etc.

3. **Character Constant:**
- A character constants can contain or store only a single character enclosed in apostrophes (single quotation marks).
    Example: 'x'   'a'   'M'   '6'   '$'
- The value of the character constant is the corresponding numeric value of the character. So, we can compare the two characters using numeric as ASCII value.

4. **String Constants:**
- A string constant is a set of characters enclosed in double quotes.
- C allows us to define string constants, it does not formally have a string data type.
    Example: "Let us learn C"
                   "123 – 45"
                   "Welcome to \n BCA Semester II"

Backslash Characters/Escape Sequences:
- C supports some special escape sequence characters that are used to do special tasks. These are also called as 'Backslash characters'.

- Table 1.1 shows blackslash characters/escape sequences.

Table 1.1

Character constant	Meaning
\n	New line (Line break)
\b	Backspace
\t	Horizontal Tab
\f	Form feed
\a	Alert (alerts a bell)
\r	Carriage Return
\v	Vertical Tab
\?	Question Mark
\'	Single Quote
\"	Double Quote
\\	Backslash
\0	Null

1.4.6 Variables

- A variable is a name assigned to the memory location where data is stored. In other words, variable is the data name that refers to the stored value.
- Variables are memory location in computer's memory to store data. To indicate the memory location, each variable should be given a unique name called identifier.
- Fig. 1.4 shows a variable num, with value 10 and memory address (location 2000).

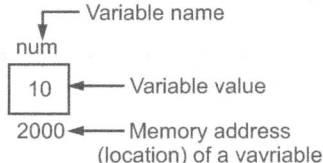

Fig. 1.4: Variables

Rules for naming variable:

1. Variable name must begin with letter or underscore.
2. Variables are case sensitive.
3. They can be constructed with digits, letters.
4. No special symbols are allowed other than underscore.
5. The variable name can contain maximum 31 characters.

1.4.6.1 Declaring and Initializing Variables

- Variables should be declared in the C program before to use. Memory space is not allocated for a variable while declaration. It happens only on variable definition.
- Variable initialization means assigning a value to the variable.

	Type	Syntax	Example
1.	Variable declaration	`data_type variable_name;`	`int x, y, z; char flat, ch;`
2.	Variable initialization	`data_type variable_name = value;`	`int x = 50, y = 30; char flag = 'x', ch='l';`

Difference between Variable Declaration and Definition:

Variable declaration	Variable definition
1. Declaration tells the compiler about data type and size of the variable.	1. Definition allocates memory for the variable.
2. Variable can be declared many times in a program.	2. It can happen only one time for a variable in a program.
3. The assignment of properties and identification to a variable.	3. Assignments of storage space to a variable.

1.4.6.2 Types of Variables

- There are two types of variables i.e., local and global variables.

1. Local Variables:

- Variables that are declared inside a function are called local variables.
- Local variables can be used only by the statement which is inside the block and in which variables are declared.
- Local variables cannot be used outside the block. Lifetime of the local variable is till the end of the block i.e. a local variable is created when block enters and destroyed when block exit.
- We can declare same variable name within two different blocks. However, we cannot have same variable name within one block.

Program 1.1: Program for local variables.
```
#include <stdio.h>
int main()
{
   int m=40,n=20;      // m, n are local variables
   if (m == n)
   {
      printf("m and n are equal");
   }
   else
   {
      printf("m and n are not equal");
   }
   return 0;
}
```
Output:
m and n are not equal

Formal Parameters:
- If a function is to use arguments, it must declare variables so that the variables will accept the values of the arguments. These variables are referred as formal parameters of the function.
- Formal parameters are local to function.

    Example:
```
double addition(int x, int y)
{
   double Z;
   Z = x + y;
   return Z;
}
```
- The function addition has two parameters x and y. This function returns addition of x and y.

2. Global Variables:
- Global variables are used anywhere in the program and they will hold their values throughout the program execution.
- Global variables are declare outside of the function.

Program 1.2: Program for global variables.
```
#include <stdio.h>
int n=20;               // n is global variable
int main()
{
   int m=40;            // m is local variable
   if (m == n)
   {
      printf("m and n are equal");
   }
   else
   {
      printf("m and n are not equal");
   }
   return 0;
}
```
Output:
```
m and n are not equal
```

- Normally, global variables are declared at the top of the program. Global variables are helpful when many functions in your program use the same data.
- Global variables are stored in a fixed region of memory and they take up memory the entire time your program is executing, not just when they are needed.

1.4.7 Data Types

- Data types are the keywords, which are used for assigning a type to a variable.
- **Definition:** "The data storage format that a variable can store a data to perform a specific operation".

OR

- Data type can be defined as "the type of data of variable or constant store."
- Data types are used to define a variable before to use in a program. Size of variable, constant and array are determined by data types.
- When we use a variable in a program then we have to mention the type of data. This can be handled using data type in C.
- Fig. 1.5 shows datatypes in C language.
   1. **Primitive data types** are the first form – the basic data types (int, char, float, double).
   2. **Derived data types** are a derivative of primitive data types known as arrays, pointer and function.
   3. **User defined** data types are those data types which are defined by the user/programmer himself.

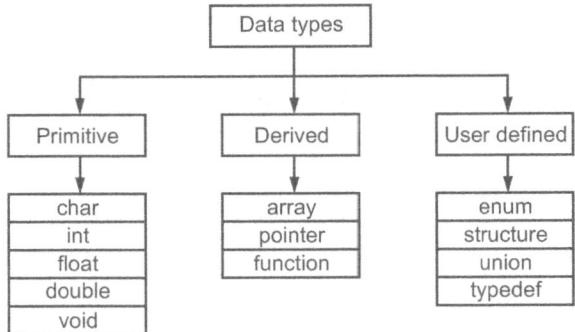

Fig. 1.5: Datatypes in C Language

1. **Simple / Built-in / Fundamental Data Types:**
   - Built-in Fundamental data types are atomic types Built-in types are also referred as **'Primitive'** data types.
   - Table 1.2 shows the most commonly used data types in C.

Table 1.2

Keyword	Format (Access) Specifier	Size	Data Range
char	%c	1 Byte	-128 to +127
unsigned char	<-- -- >	8 Bytes	0 to 255
int	%d	2 Bytes	-32768 to +32767
long int	%ld	4 Bytes	-231 to +231
unsigned int	%u	2 Bytes	0 to 65535
float	%f	4 Bytes	-3.4e38 to +3.4e38
double	%lf	8 Bytes	-1.7e38 to +1.7e38
long double	%Lf	12-16 Bytes	-3.4e38 to +3.4e38

(i) **Integer:** Integer data type is simply written as **int**. To store the integer i.e. whole number, typical memory requirement is 1 word or 2 bytes, (1 byte consists of 8 bits). They can be further of the type: long int, short int, signed int, unsigned int, these are called as **qualifiers**.

(ii) **Character:** This is used when we deal with character type of data containing a – z or A – Z characters available in C character set.

(iii) **Float:** It is also used to store numeric data only the difference is that here we can also use numeric data having decimal values. Some compilers permits use of long, float, short float etc.

(iv) **Double:** If we use exponential in the programme then it forms a very long number. So we use type double.

(v) Void: Using void data type, we can specify the type of a function. It is a good practice to avoid functions that does not return any values to the calling function. Void is empty data type.

Example:
(i) `void func1 (int x)`
   Here, func1 does not return any value.
(ii) `int func2 (void)`
   We can use void as a data type as parameter list.

2. **Derived Data Types:**
- The data types which are derived from built-in or primitive data types are called as derived data types.
- These data types can be derived using declaration operators are punctuators.
   (i) Array: An array is a derived data type as it can be derived from built-in data types. It is basically a named, consecutive and finite set of memory locations, which can hold multiple data items of its declared data type.

   Example:
   - `int ARR[5],` /*Here ARR is an array of type integer having 5(0 to 4) consecutive memory blocks*/
   - `float ARR[5],` /*Here ARR is an array of type floating-point having 5(0 to 4) consecutive memory blocks*/

   (ii) Functions: A function in C is a named and finite set of C program statements. They are designed to do some specific task or to take some specific actions. Functions are associated with return types, actual and formal argument list. Typically a function is associated with three tasks.
   - Function prototyping,
   - Function definition writing, and
   - Function calling.

   (iii) Pointers: A pointer is a special variable which holds the address of a normal variable of its own data type. The pointer variable can be declared with the help of a punctuator *(astrick).

   Example:
   ```
   int *ptr,   /*declared a pointer variable named as 'ptr' and is
               of type 'int' */
   int num;
   ptr = &num; /*assigned the address of variable 'num' of type
               'int' to the pointer variable */
   ```

3. **User Defined Types:**
- User defined data types are the customized data type. It can be composed of variety of the built-in and derived data types (excluding function).
- A user-defined data type is specially designed to meet once programming needs.

- In C language, the user defined data types are created using:
  - **(i) Enum Data Type:** This is an user defined data type having finite set of enumeration constants. The keyword 'enum' is used to create enumerated data type.
    Syntax: `enum [data_type] {const1, const2, ...., const n};`
    Example: `enum mca(software, web, seo);`
  - **(ii) typedef:** It is used to create new data type. But it is commonly used to change existing data type with another name.
    Syntax: `typedef [data_type] synonym;`
    OR
    `typedef [data_type] new_data_type;`
    Example: `typedef int integer;`
    `integer rno;`
  - **(iii) Structure:** A structure is composed of one or more built-in or/and derived data types (excluding function). Every element of the structure has separate storage space. So the size of a variable of structure type will have the memory space equal to the sum of memory spaces of its all individual elements. Keyword struct is used define a structure.
  - **(iv) Union:** A union is also composed of one or more built-in and/or derived data types (excluding function). Keyword union is used to define a unions.

1.5 Operators

- Operators are the symbol which operates a value or a variable.
- Operators represent an operation.
- The symbols which are used to perform logical and mathematical operations are called operators.
- C is very rich in built-in operations. Operators instruct the compiler to perform some actions on operands.
- An operator can be unary (one operand), binary (two operands) or ternary (three operand).
  Example: unary   – 5
  binary   3 + 2
  ternary   conditional operators
             (a > b) ? a: b

1.5.1 Types of Operators

1. Arithmetic Operators:
- It is also called as 'binary operators'. It is used to perform arithmetical operations. These operators operate on two operands.

- Following are arithmetic operators supported by C language and assume variable A holds 10 and variable B holds 20 then:

Operator	Description	Example
+	Adds two operands.	A + B will give 30
-	Subtracts second operand from the first.	A - B will give -10
*	Multiply both operands.	A * B will give 200
/	Divide numerator by enumerators.	B / A will give 2
%	Modulus Operator and remainder of after an integer division.	B % A will give 0
++	Increment operator, increases integer value by one.	A++ will give 11
--	Decrement operator, decreases integer value by one.	A-- will give 9

Program 1.3: Program for arithmetic operators.

```
#include <stdio.h>
void main()
{
    int a = 21;
    int b = 10;
    int c ;
    c = a + b;
    printf("Value of c is %d\n", c );
    c = a - b;
    printf("Value of c is %d\n", c );
    c = a * b;
    printf("Value of c is %d\n", c );
    c = a / b;
    printf("Value of c is %d\n", c );
    c = a % b;
    printf("Value of c is %d\n", c );
    c = a++;
    printf("Value of c is %d\n", c );
    c = a--;
    printf("Value of c is %d\n", c );
}
```

Output:

```
Value of c is 31
Value of c is 11
Value of c is 210
Value of c is 2
Value of c is 1
Value of c is 21
Value of c is 22
```

2. **Relational and Logical Operators:**
- Relational operators used in expressions and result of expression are either true (1) or false (0).
- Logical operators are used to perform logical operations on the given two variables.
- There are following relational operators supported by C language. Assume variable A holds 10 and variable B holds 20 then:

Relational Operator	Description	Example
==	Checks if the value of two operands is equal or not, if yes then condition becomes true.	(A == B) is false.
!=	Checks if the value of two operands is equal or not, if values are not equal then condition becomes true.	(A != B) is true.
>	Checks if the value of left operand is greater than the value of right operand, if yes then condition becomes true.	(A > B) is false.
<	Checks if the value of left operand is less than the value of right operand, if yes then condition becomes true.	(A < B) is true.
>=	Checks if the value of left operand is greater than or equal to the value of right operand, if yes then condition becomes true.	(A >= B) is false.
<=	Checks if the value of left operand is less than or equal to the value of right operand, if yes then condition becomes true.	(A <= B) is true.

- Following table shows various logical operations.

Logical Operator	Description	Example
&& (Logical AND operator)	If both the operands are non zero then condition becomes true.	(A && B) is true.
|| (Logical OR Operator)	If any of the two operands is non zero then condition becomes true.	(A || B) is true.
! (Logical NOT Operator)	Use to reverses the logical state of its operand. If a condition is true then Logical NOT operator will make false.	!(A && B) is false.

Program 1.4: Program for relational operators.

```
#include <stdio.h>
void main()
{
    int a = 21;
    int b = 10;
    int c ;
    if( a == b )
    {
        printf("a is equal to b\n" );
    }
    else
    {
        printf("a is not equal to b\n" );
    }
    if ( a < b )
    {
        printf("a is less than b\n" );
    }
    else
    {
        printf("a is not less than b\n" );
    }
```

```c
        if ( a > b )
        {
            printf("a is greater than b\n" );
        }
        else
        {
            printf("a is not greater than b\n" );
        }
        /* Lets change value of a and b */
        a = 5;
        b = 20;
        if ( a <= b )
        {
            printf("a is either less than or equal to  b\n" );
        }
        if ( b >= a )
        {
            printf("b is either greater than  or equal to a\n" );
        }
    }
```

Output:
```
a is not equal to b
a is not less than b
a is greater than b
a is either less than or equal to  b
b is either greater than  or equal to a
```

Program 1.5: Program for logical operators.

```c
    #include <stdio.h>
    void main()
    {
        int a = 5;
        int b = 20;
        int c ;
        if ( a && b )
        {
            printf("Condition is true\n" );
        }
```

```c
    if ( a || b )
    {
       printf("Condition is true\n" );
    }
    /* lets change the value of  a and b */
    a = 0;
    b = 10;
    if ( a && b )
    {
       printf("Condition is true\n" );
    }
    else
    {
       printf("Condition is not true\n" );
    }
    if ( !(a && b) )
    {
       printf("Condition is true\n" );
    }
 }
```

Output:
```
Condition is true
Condition is true
Condition is not true
Condition is true
```

3. **Assignment Operators:**
- These operators are used to assign a value to variable.
- There are following assignment operators supported by C language:

Operator	Description	Example
= (Simple assignment operator)	Assigns values from right side operands to left side operand.	C = A + B will assigne value of A + B into C
+= (Add AND assignment operator)	It adds right operand to the left operand and assign the result to left operand.	C += A is equivalent to C = C + A

contd. ...

-= (Subtract AND assignment operator)	It subtracts right operand from the left operand and assign the result to left operand.	C -= A is equivalent to C = C - A
*= (Multiply AND assignment operator)	It multiplies right operand with the left operand and assign the result to left operand.	C *= A is equivalent to C = C * A
/= (Divide AND assignment operator)	It divides left operand with the right operand and assign the result to left operand.	C /= A is equivalent to C = C / A
%= (Modulus AND assignment operator)	It takes modulus using two operands and assign the result to left operand.	C %= A is equivalent to C = C % A
<<=	Left shift AND assignment operator.	C <<= 2 is same as C = C << 2
>>=	Right shift AND assignment operator.	C >>= 2 is same as C = C >> 2
&=	Bitwise AND assignment operator.	C &= 2 is same as C = C & 2
^=	bitwise exclusive OR and assignment operator.	C ^= 2 is same as C = C ^ 2
|=	bitwise inclusive OR and assignment operator.	C |= 2 is same as C = C | 2

Program 1.6: Program for assignment operators.

```
#include <stdio.h>
void main()
{
   int a = 21;
   int c ;
   c =  a;
   printf("Value of c = %d\n", c );
   c +=  a;
   printf("Value of c = %d\n", c );
   c -=  a;
   printf("Value of c = %d\n", c );
   c *=  a;
```

```
        printf("Value of c = %d\n", c );
        c /=  a;
        printf("Value of c = %d\n", c );
        c  = 200;
        c %=  a;
        printf("Value of c = %d\n", c );
        c <<=  2;
        printf("Value of c = %d\n", c );
        c >>=  2;
        printf("Value of c = %d\n", c );
        c &=  2;
        printf("Value of c = %d\n", c );
        c ^=  2;
        printf("Value of c = %d\n", c );
        c |=  2;
        printf("Value of c = %d\n", c );
    }
```
Output:
```
    Value of c = 21
    Value of c = 42
    Value of c = 21
    Value of c = 441
    Value of c = 21
    Value of c = 11
    Value of c = 44
    Value of c = 11
    Value of c = 2
    Value of c = 0
    Value of c = 2
```

4. Bitwise Operators:
- Bitwise operator works on bits and performs bit by bit operation.
- Bitwise operators are used for manipulation of data at a bit level.
- They can be directly applied to char, short int and long.
- Assume if A = 60; and B = 13; Now in binary format they will be as follows:
    A = 0011 1100
    B = 0000 1101

    A&B = 0000 1100
    A|B = 0011 1101
    A^B = 0011 0001
    ~A = 1100 0011

- There are following Bitwise operators supported by C language.

Operator	Description	Example
& (Binary AND Operator)	Copies a bit to the result if it exists in both operands.	(A & B) will give 12 which is 0000 1100
| (Binary OR Operator)	Copies a bit if it exists in eather operand.	(A | B) will give 61 which is 0011 1101
^ (Binary XOR Operator)	Copies the bit if it is set in one operand but not both.	(A ^ B) will give 49 which is 0011 0001
~ (Binary Ones Complement Operator)	Is unary and has the efect of 'flipping' bits.	(~A) will give -60 which is 1100 0011
<< (Binary Left Shift Operator)	The left operands value is moved left by the number of bits specified by the right operand.	A << 2 will give 240 which is 1111 0000
>> (Binary Right Shift Operator)	The left operands value is moved right by the number of bits specified by the right operand.	A >> 2 will give 15 which is 0000 1111

Program 1.7: Program for bitwise operators.

```c
#include <stdio.h>
void main()
{
   unsigned int a = 60; /* 60 = 0011 1100 */
   unsigned int b = 13; /* 13 = 0000 1101 */
   int c = 0;
   c = a & b;       /* 12 = 0000 1100 */
   printf("Value of c is %d\n", c );
   c = a | b;       /* 61 = 0011 1101 */
   printf("Value of c is %d\n", c );
   c = a ^ b;       /* 49 = 0011 0001 */
   printf("Value of c is %d\n", c );
   c = ~a;          /*-61 = 1100 0011 */
   printf("Value of c is %d\n", c );
   c = a << 2;      /* 240 = 1111 0000 */
   printf("Value of c is %d\n", c );
   c = a >> 2;      /* 15 = 0000 1111 */
   printf("Value of c is %d\n", c );
}
```

Output:
```
Value of c is 12
Value of c is 61
Value of c is 49
Value of c is -61
Value of c is 240
Value of c is 15
```

5. **Other Operators:**
- There are few other operators supported by C Language.

Operator	Description	Example
sizeof()	Returns the size of an variable.	sizeof(a), where a is interger, will return 4.
&	Returns the address of an variable.	&a; will give actaul address of the variable.
*	Pointer to a variable.	*a; will pointer to a variable.
?:	Conditional Expression	If Condition is true ? Then value X: Otherwise value Y
,	Comma Operator	Used to separate set of expressions.

Program 1.8: Program for sizeof operator.
```
#include <stdio.h>
int main()
{
    int a;
    float b;
    double c;
    char d;
    printf("Size of int=%d bytes\n",sizeof(a));
    printf("Size of float=%d bytes\n",sizeof(b));
    printf("Size of double=%d bytes\n",sizeof(c));
    printf("Size of char=%d byte\n",sizeof(d));
    return 0;
}
```
Output:
```
Size of int=2 bytes
Size of float=4 bytes
Size of double=8 bytes
Size of char=1 byte
```

Program 1.9: Program for conditional operator.

```
#include <stdio.h>
int main()
{
    char feb;
    int days;
    printf("Enter l if the year is leap year otherwise enter 0: ");
    scanf("%c",&feb);
    days=(feb=='l')?29:28;
    /*If test condition (feb=='l') is true, days will be equal to 29. */
    /*If test condition (feb=='l') is false, days will be equal to 28. */
    printf("Number of days in February = %d",days);
    return 0;
}
```

Output:
```
Enter l if the year is leap year otherwise enter n: l
Number of days in February = 29
```

1.5.2 Precedence and Associativity of Operators

1. **Precedence of operators:**
- If more than one operators are involved in an expression then, C language has predefined rule of priority of operators. This rule of priority of operators is called operator precedence.
- In C, precedence of arithmetic operators (*,%,/,+,-) is higher than relational operators (==,!=,>,<,>=,<=) and precedence of relational operator is higher than logical operators (&&, || and !).

2. **Associativity of operators:**
- Associativity indicates in which order two operators of same precedence (priority) executes. Let us suppose an expression:

    a==b!=c

- Here, operators == and != have same precedence. The associativity of both == and != is left to right, i.e, the expression in left is executed first and execution take pale towards right. Thus, a==b!=c equivalent to:

    (a==b)!=c

- The Table 1.3 below shows all the operators in C with precedence and associativity.

Table 1.3

Operator	Meaning of Operator	Associativity
() [] -> .	Functional call Array element reference Indirect member selection Direct member selection	Left to right
! ~ + − ++ − − & * sizeof (type)	Logical negation Bitwise (1's) complement Unary plus Unary minus Increment Decrement Dereference Operator (Address) Pointer reference Returns the size of an object Type cast (conversion)	Right to left
* / %	Multiply Divide Remainder	Left to right
+ −	Binary plus (Addition) Binary minus (Subtraction)	Left to right
<< >>	Left shift Right shift	Left to right
< <= > >=	Less than Less than or equal Greater than Greater than or equal	Left to right
== !=	Equal to Not equal to	Left to right
&	Bitwise AND	Left to right
^	Bitwise exclusive OR	Left to right
|	Bitwise OR	Left to right

contd. ...

&&	Logical AND		Left to right
||	Logical OR		Left to right
?:	Conditional Operator		Left to right
=	Simple assignment		
*=	Assign product		
/=	Assign quotient		
%=	Assign remainder		
-=	Assign sum		Right to left
&=	Assign difference		
^=	Assign bitwise AND		
|=	Assign bitwise XOR		
<<=	Assign bitwise OR		
>>=	Assign left shift		
	Assign right shift		
,	Separator of expressions		Left to right

1.5.3 Expressions

- An expression in C is a combination of constants, functions and variables written according to the syntax of language.
- We can define expression as "A series of variables, operators and constants calls that evaluates to a single value".
- Expressions perform the work of a program.
- Expressions are evaluated using precedence of operators.
- When the variables of different types are mixed in an expression, they are all converted to the same type.
- Examples of expressions in C are given below:

    z = x + y

    a = b

    c = a + b;

    a < = b;

    c = = d;

Questions

1. What is C language? Enlist its features.
2. With the help of diagram describe history of C language.
3. State various advantages and disadvantages of C language.
4. Explain basic structure of C programming diagrammatically.
5. Write short note on:
   (i) Character set.
   (ii) Operators.
6. What is meant by token? Explain its types.
7. Define the following terms:
   (i) Identifier.
   (ii) Constant.
   (iii) Expressions.
8. What are the types of operators in C language? Explain two of them in detail.
9. What is variable? List types of variables.
10. How to declare and define variable? Explain with example.
11. Write short note on: Precedence and associativity of operators.
12. What is keyword? Enlist any eight keywords in C language.
13. Write a program to add three number using arithmetic operators.
14. Write a program to find greatest number among four numbers.
15. Differentiate between global and local variables.
16. Define datatype. Enlist various types of data types is C language.
17. Give the outputs of following:
    (i)
    ```
    main()
    {
      int x = 20 * 30, y;
      y = x/2
      printf("%d %d", x, y);
    }
    ```
    (ii)
    ```
    main()
    {
      int a, b, c;
      a = b = c = - 1
      cx = ++ d && ++b || c;
      printf ("a = %d, b = %d, c = %d, a, b, c);
    }
    ```

(iii) main()
```
{
    char ch = 'X''
    int i = 2;
    float f = ++ch +i;}
    printf("%f %d %c, f, ch, ch);
}
```
(iv) main()
```
{
    const int a;
    a = 130;
    printf("%d", a);
}
```

Chapter 2...

Managing I/O Operations

Contents ...
2.1 Introduction
2.2 Console based I/O and Related Built-in I/O Functions
    2.2.1 printf() Function
    2.2.2 scanf() Function
    2.2.3 getchar() Function
    2.2.4 getch() Function
2.3 Formatted Input and Output Functions
- Questions

2.1 Introduction

- In C, Input and Output operations are perform using library function – without these functions we cannot interact with the compiler.
- We can perform input functions using input device i.e. keyboard and output functions using output devices i.e. screen or printer and having interaction with compiler through these devices.
- There are both console and file Input/Output (I/O) functions. Here, we refers to the console I/O functions as performing input from the keyboard and output to the screen.
- To use all these I/O functions we have to include as important header file **stdio.h** using statement, #include<stdio.h> this statement is included before every program.
- There are numerous library functions available for I/O. These can be classified into two broad categories:
    1. **Console I/O functions:** Functions to receive input from keyboard and write output to VDU.
    2. **File I/O functions:** Functions to perform I/O operations on a floppy disk or hard disk.

2.2 Console based I/O and Related Built-in I/O Functions

- The screen and keyboard together are called a console. Console I/O functions can be further classified into two categories— formatted and unformatted console I/O functions.
- The functions available under each of these two categories are shown in Fig. 2.1.

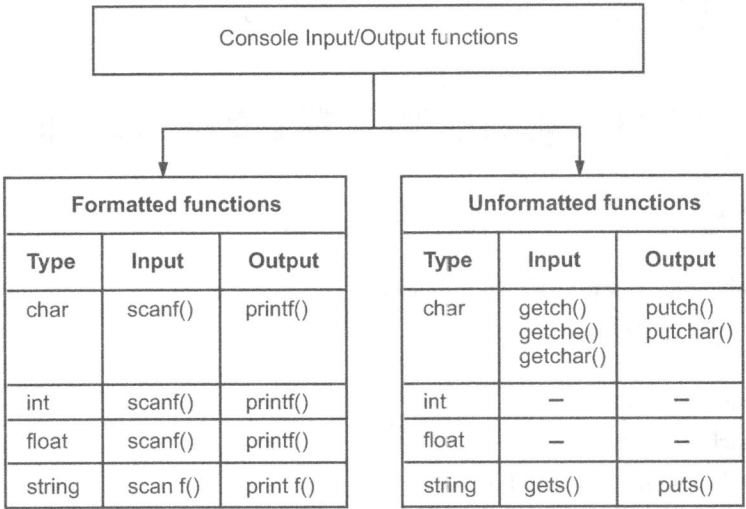

Fig. 2.1: Function categories

2.2.1 printf() Function

- printf() function is used to display output of a program on screen.
- printf () is one of the library function.

    Syntax: `printf("information string", arg1, arg2, ... , argn)`

    where, information string refer to a string that containing formatting information and arg1, arg2, ...argn are arguments that represent the individual output data items.

- Escape sequence is a pair of character. The first letter is a slash followed by a character. Escape sequence help us to represent within the format string invisible and non-printed character although there are physically two characters in any escape sequence. It actually represents only one.
- The various escape sequences are:

1.	\n	New line
2.	\t	Tab
3.	\b	Back space
4.	\a	Bell
5.	\o	Null character
6.	\?	To print question mark
7.	\\	To print slash
8.	\'	To print single quote
9.	\"	To print double quote

- The Conversion specification inscribes the printf() function that it could print some value at that location in the text.

- Format (Access) Specifiers are:

%d	Data item is displayed as a signed decimal integer.
%i	Data item is displayed as a single decimal integer.
%f	Data item is displayed as a floating-point value without an exponent.
%c	Data item is displayed as a single character.
%e	Data item is displayed as a floating-point value with an exponent.
%g	Data item is displayed as a floating-point value using either e-type or f-type conversion depending on value.
%o	Data item is displayed as an octal integer, without a leading zero.
%s	Data item is displayed as string.
%u	Data item is displayed as an unsigned decimal integer.
%x	Data item is displayed as a hexadecimal integer, without a leading 0x.

Program 2.1: Program for C printf().

```
#include <stdio.h>
int main()
{
    char ch;
    char str[100];
    printf("Enter any character \n");
    scanf("%c", &ch);
    printf("Entered character is %c \n", ch);
    printf("Enter any string ( upto 100 character ) \n");
    scanf("%s", &str);
    printf("Entered string is %s \n", str);
    return 0;
}
```

Output:
```
Enter any character
a
Entered character is a
Enter any string ( upto 100 character )
hai
Entered string is hai
```

- The format specifier %c is used in scanf statement so that the value entered is received as an character and %s for string.

2.2.2 scanf() Function

- To read data from the user we use scanf().
- The scanf( ) is used to read all the built-in data types and automatically convert numbers into the proper internal format.
- scanf() is the general purpose console input routine.

  Syntax: `scanf("information string", arg1, arg2, ...... argn);`

  where, information string consists of, format specifiers, white space characters (tab, newline, blank), non-white-space characters which causes scanf to discard the matching character etc.

  Example: `scanf("%d", &a);`

- Here, we consider a is integer, so we use %d and a value will be read from keyboard and this will automatically given to a, Also &a reserves the memory location for the value.

Program 2.2: Program to find average of three subject of student.

```c
#include<stdio.h>
void main( )
{
   char name[30] ;
   int a, b, c ;
   float result ;
   printf("\n please enter name:") ;
   scanf (" %s", name) ;
   printf("\n please enter mark 1:") ;
   scanf (" %d", &a);
   printf(" \n please enter mark 2: ") ;
   scanf ("%d", &b);
   printf ("\n Please enter mark 3: ");
   scanf("%d", &c);
   result = (a + b + c)/3 ;
   printf("\n average = %f", result) ;
   getch( ) ;
}
```

Output:
```
Please enter name        :   Omkar
Please enter mark 1      :   80
Please enter mark 2      :   75
Please enter mark 3      :   60
average = 71.0000
```

2.2.3 getchar() Function

- getchar() is used to get or read the input (i.e a single character) at run time.
  Syntax: `int getchar(void);`
  Example:
  ```
  void main()
  {
  char ch;
  ch = getchar();
  printf("Input Char Is:%c",ch);
  }
  ```

Program Explanation:
- Here, declare the variable **ch** as char data type, and then get a value through getchar() library function and store it in the variable ch. And then, print the value of variable ch.
- During the program execution, a single character is get or read through the **getchar()**. The given value is displayed on the screen and the compiler wait for another character to be typed. If you press the enter key/any other characters and then only the given character is printed through the **printf** function.

2.2.4 getch() Function

- getch() is used to get a character from console but does not echo to the screen.
  Syntax: `int getch(void);`
- getch() reads a single character directly from the keyboard, without echoing to the screen.
  ```
  void main()
  {
      char ch;
      ch = getch();
      printf("Input Char Is:%c",ch);
  }
  ```

Program Explanation:
- Here, declare the variable **ch** as char data type, and then get a value through getch() library function and store it in the variable ch. And then, print the value of variable ch.
- During the program execution, a single character is get or read through the **getch()**. The given value is not displayed on the screen and the compiler does not wait for another character to be typed. And then, the given character is printed through the **printf** function.

2.3 Formatted Input and Output Functions

1. getche() Function:
- getche() is used to get a character from console, and echoes to the screen.
  Syntax: `int getche(void);`
- getche reads a single character from the keyboard and echoes it to the current text window, using direct video or BIOS.

Example:
```
void main()
{
    char ch;
    ch = getche();
    printf("Input Char Is:%c",ch);
}
```

Program Explanation:
- Here, declare the variable **ch** as char data type, and then get a value through **getche()** library function and store it in the variable **ch**. And then, print the value of variable **ch**.
- During the program execution, a single character is get or read through the **getche()**. The given value is displayed on the screen and the compiler does not wait for another character to be typed. Then, after wards the character is printed through the **printf** function.

2. **sprintf( ) Function:**
- The sprintf function converts, formats, and stores its value parameters, under control of the format parameter.

    Syntax: `str=sprintf(format,value_1,..,value_n)`
- Parameters:
    - **format:** a Scilab string. Specifies a character string combining literal characters with conversion specifications.
    - **value_n:** Specifies the data to be converted according to the format parameter.
    - **str:** column vector of character strings.

    The format parameter is a character string that contains two types of objects:
    - **Literal characters:** which are copied to the output stream.
    - **Conversion specifications:** each of which causes zero or more items to be fetched from the value parameter list.

3. **sscanf( ) Function:**
- sscanf() converts formatted input given by a string. The sscanf functions interpret character string according to a format, and returns the converted results. The format parameter contains conversion specifications used to interpret the input.
- The format parameter can contain white-space characters (blanks, tabs, newline, or formfeed) that, except in the following two cases, read the input up to the next nonwhite-space character.
- Unless there is a match in the control string, trailing white space (including a newline character) is not read.
    1. Any character except % (percent sign), which must match the next character of the input stream.
    2. A conversion specification that directs the conversion of the next input field.

    Syntax: `[v_1,...v_n]=sscanf (string,format)`

- Parameters:
  - **format:** Specifies the format conversion.
  - **string:** Specifies input to be read.

4. **String Input and Output functions:**
- The functions gets() and puts() used for string reading (input) and string writing (output) purpose from standard library functions.

(i) gets() Function:
- This function reads a string of characters entered at the keyboard. You can type the characters at the keyboard until a carriage return or ENTER is pressed.
- The end of string is denoted by null character (\0) whitespaces (tab and spaces) are allows in a string.

Syntax: gets(string_name)

Program 2.3: Program for gets().
```
#include<stdio.h>
void main()
{
char str[80];
gets(str);
}
```

- So from the above program we have demonstrated the use of gets(). The scanning or reading the string from keyboard continues till the <Enter> key is pressed.

(ii) puts() Function:
- This function is use to print a string on the screen. It is equivalent to printf() function, but in printf statement we can display messages along with printing at the same time.
- The puts() function can only output a string of characters, it cannot output numbers or do format conversions. Therefore, puts() requires less space than printf() and also it runs faster than printf().

Syntax: puts(string_name)

Program 2.4: Program for puts().
```
#include<stdio.h>
void main()
{
    char str[80];
    gets(str);
    puts(str);
    printf("The line is: %s", str);
}
```

Output:
```
This is my string data
This is my string data
The line is: This is my string data (writing by printf)
```

- So we can see that the main use of gets and puts is to transfer the line of text to and from the computer.

5. putchar() Function:
- The putchar() function writes a character to the screen at the current cursor position. We can return a single character and print it on the screen.

   Syntax: putchar (char_variable);
- The value of char_variable is print on the screen.

Program 2.5: Program to calculate area of circle (formula: $\pi * r * r$).

```c
#include<stdio.h>
#include<conio.h>
void main()
{
   float radius,area;
   clrscr(); // Clear Screen
   printf("\n Enter the radius of Circle: ");
   scanf("%f",&radius);
   area = 3.14 * radius * radius;
   printf("\n Area of Circle: %f",area);
   getch();
}
```

Output:
```
Enter the radius of Circle: 2.0
Area of Circle: 12.56
```

Program 2.6: Program to calculate area of square, (Formula area: side * side).

```c
#include<stdio.h>
#include<conio.h>
void main()
{
   int side,area;
   clrscr(); // Clear Screen
   printf("\n Enter the Length of Side: ");
   scanf("%d",&side);
   area = side * side ;
   printf("\n Area of Square: %d",area);
   getch();
}
```

Output:
```
Enter the Length of Side: 4
Area of Square: 16
```

Program 2.7: Program to calculate area of rectangle (Formula: area = l * b).
```
#include<stdio.h>
#include<conio.h>
void main()
{
int length,breadth,side, area;
clrscr(); // Clear Screen
printf("\n Enter the Length of Rectangle: ");
scanf("%d",&length);
printf("\n Enter the Breadth of Rectangle: ");
scanf("%d",&breadth);
area = length * breadth;
printf("\n Area of Rectangle: %d",area);
getch();
}
```
Output:
```
Enter the Length of Rectangle: 5
Enter the Breadth of Rectangle: 6
Area of Rectangle: 30
```

Program 2.8: Program to convert temperature fahrenheit into celsius.
```
#include<stdio.h>
#include<conio.h>
void main()
{
 float Fahrenheit, Celsius;
 clrscr();
 printf("Enter Temperature in Fahrenheit \n");
 scanf("%f",&Fahrenheit);
 Celsius = 5.0/9.0 * (Fahrenheit-32);
 printf("\n Temperature in Fahrenheit = %f", Fahrenheit);
 printf("\n Temperature in Celsius = %f", Celsius);
 getch();
}
```
Output:
```
Enter Temperature in Fahrenheit
15.2
Temperature in Fahrenheit = 15.2000
Temperature in Celsius = -9.3333
```

Questions

1. What is meant by built-in I/O functions?
2. Which header file is use for input-output operations?
3. State two functions for reading the characteristics from the user.
4. What is the difference between puts() and putchar().
5. What is a purpose of scanf() function? State any four format specifies used with scanf().
6. What is the purpose of printf() function? State any four format specifiers used in printf( ) statement with an example.
7. Write a program to find the area of a rectangle.
8. Write a program to find volume of a cylinder.
9. Write a program to convert an upper case character to lower case.
10. Write a program to find cube of a number.
11. Write a program to find sine of an angle.
12. What will be the values stored in the variables total and item_code when the data 1500, P is keyed in as a response to the following statements:
    (a) scanf("%d %c", &total, &item_code);
    (b) scanf("%d %s", &total, &item_code);
    (c) scanf("%c %d", &total, &item_code);
    (d) scanf("%d %c", &item_code, &total);
13. What is the difference between putchar() and getchar().

■■■

Chapter 3...

Decision Making and Looping

Contents ...

3.1 Introduction

3.2 Decision Making Structure

    3.2.1 if Statement

    3.2.2 if-else Statement

    3.2.3 Nested if-else Statement

    3.2.4 switch Statement

    3.2.5 Conditional Operator

3.3 Loops

    3.3.1 for Loop

    3.3.2 while Loop

    3.3.3 do-while Loop

3.4 Jump Statements

    3.4.1 goto Statement

    3.4.2 break Statement

    3.4.3 continue Statement

    3.4.4 exit() Function

- Questions

3.1 Introduction

- Decision making structures require that the programmer specify one or more conditions to be evaluated or tested by the program, along with a statement or statements to be executed if the condition is determined to be true, and optionally, other statements to be executed if the condition is determined to be false.
- Fig. 3.1 shows the general from of a typical decision making structure found in most of the programming languages.

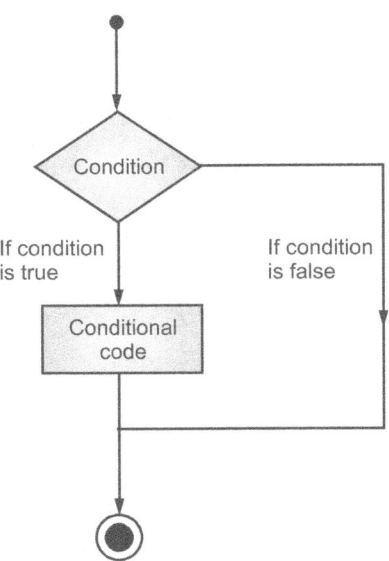

Fig. 3.1

- C programming language assumes any non-zero and non-null values as true and if it is either zero or null then it is assumed as false value.
- C programming language provides following types of decision making statements.

Statement	Description
1. if statement	An if statement consists of a boolean expression followed by one or more statements.
2. if...else statement	An if statement can be followed by an optional else statement, which executes when the boolean expression is false.
3. nested if statements	You can use one if or else if statement inside another if or else if statements.
4. switch statement	A switch statement allows a variable to be tested for equality against a list of values.
5. nested switch statements	You can use one switch statement inside another switch statements.

- There may be a situation when you need to execute a block of code several number of times. In general statements are executed sequentially: The first statement in a function is executed first, followed by the second, and so on.
- A loop statement allows us to execute a statement or group of statements multiple times. Fig. 3.2 shows the general from of a loop statement in most of the programming languages.

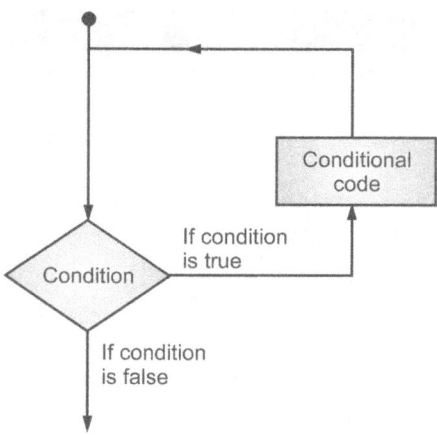

Fig. 3.2

- C programming language provides following types of loop to handle looping requirements.

Type of Loop	Description
1. while loop	Repeats a statement or group of statements while a given condition is true. It tests the condition before executing the loop body.
2. for loop	Execute a sequence of statements multiple times and abbreviates the code that manages the loop variable.
3. do...while loop	Like a while statement, except that it tests the condition at the end of the loop body

- C provides following types of statements:
  1. **Expression statement:** Number of expression statements are assignments or function calls.
  2. **Compound statement:** More than two statements grouped together in { } forms a compound statement.
  3. **Selection statement:** These statements involve condition checking and choose one of several flows of controls. if, if ... else, switch are the examples of selection statement.
  4. **Null statement:** These statements does not perform any action. A semicolon (;) on the line of code is a null statement.
  5. **Iteration statement:** These statement specify looping, where a statement has to be repeatedly executed a specific number of times as the test expression is satisfied. for, do while and while loop are the examples of iteration statement.
  6. **jump statement:** These statements transfer control unconditionality goto, break, continue are the examples of jump statements.

3.2 Decision Making Structure

- C program executes program sequentially. Sometimes, a program requires checking of certain conditions in program execution.
- C provides various key condition statements to check condition and execute statements according conditional criteria.
- These statements are called as 'Selection' or 'Conditional Statements.'
- Fig. 3.3 shows decision-making statement.

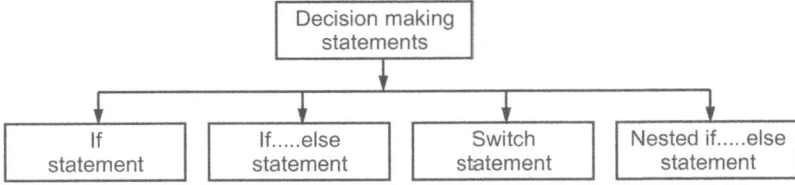

Fig. 3.3: Types of decision making statements

3.2.1 if Statement

- This is a conditional statement used in C to check condition or to control the flow of execution of statements.
- This is also called as 'decision making statement or control statement.'
- The execution of a whole program is done in one direction only.

Syntax:
```
if(condition)
{
    statements;
}
```

- In above syntax, the condition is checked first. If it is true, then the program control flow goes inside the braces and executes the block of statements associated with it. If it returns false, then program skips the braces. If there are more than 1 (one) statements in if statement then use { } braces else it is not necessary to use.
- Fig. 3.4 shows flowchart of if statement.

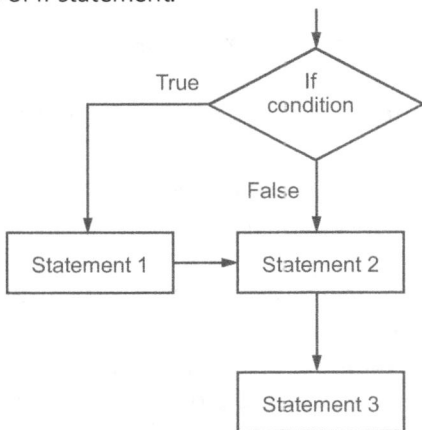

Fig. 3.4: Flowchart of if statement

- If the condition is true, the n statement 1 is executed and if false if won't be executed. Remember statements 2 and 3 are always executed.

Program 3.1: Program for if statement.
```
#include<stdio.h>
#include<conio.h>
void main()
{
   int num;
   clrscr();
   printf("\n Enter a number less than 10:");
   scanf("%d", &num);
   if(num <= 10)
   printf("\n The number is less than 10");
   getch();
}
```
Output:
First run:
```
Enter a number less than 10 : 8
The number is less than 10
```
Second run:
```
Enter a number less than 10 : 14
```
- After second run there will be no output because the condition given in the 'if' statement is false. The 'if' statements are only executed when the condition is true.

Program 3.2: C program to print the number entered by user only if the number entered is negative.
```
#include <stdio.h>
int main()
{
   int num;
   printf("Enter a number to check.\n");
   scanf("%d",&num);
   if(num<0) /* checking whether number is less than 0 or not. */
   printf("Number=%d\n",num);
   /*If test condition is true, statement above will be executed,
   otherwise it will not be executed */
   printf("The if statement in C programming is easy.");
   return 0;
}
```
Output 1:
```
Enter a number to check.
-2
Number=-2
The if statement in C programming is easy.
```

- When user enters -2 then, the test expression (num<0) becomes true. Hence, Number=-2 is displayed in the screen.

Output 2:

Enter a number to check.

5

The if statement in C programming is easy.

3.2.2 if-else Statement

- This is also one of the most useful conditional statement used in C to check conditions.
- The if statement will execute the statement if the expression is true otherwise it will be skipped.
- The if-else statement allows us to select one of the two variable options depending upon outcome of test condition.

Syntax:

```
if(condition)
{
    true statements;
}
else
{
    false statements;
}
```

- In above syntax, the condition is checked first. If it is true, then the program control flow goes inside the braces and executes the block of statements associated with it. If it returns false, then it executes the else part of a program.
- Fig. 3.5 shows flowchart for if...else statement.

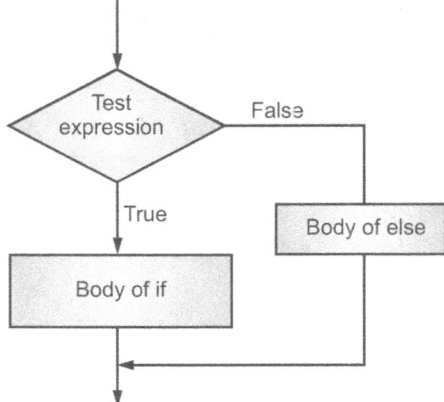

Fig. 3.5: Operation of if...else statement

Program 3.3: Program to check whether input alphabet is a vowel or not.
```c
#include <stdio.h>
int main()
{
    char ch;
    printf("Enter a character\n");
    scanf("%c", &ch);
    if (ch == 'a' || ch == 'A' || ch == 'e' || ch == 'E' || ch == 'i'
    || ch == 'I' || ch =='o' || ch=='O' || ch == 'u' || ch == 'U')
    printf("%c is a vowel.\n", ch);
    else
    printf("%c is not a vowel.\n", ch);
    return 0;
}
```
Output 1:
```
Enter a character
i
i is a vowel.
```
Output 2:
```
Enter a character
x
x is not a vowel.
```

Program 3.4: Write a C program to check whether a number entered by user is even or odd.
```c
#include <stdio.h>
int main()
{
    int num, n=0;
    printf("Enter a number you want to check.\n");
    scanf("%d",&num);
    n=num;
    if((num%2)==0) //checking whether remainder is 0 or not.
    printf("%d is even.",num);
    else
    printf("%d is odd.",num);
    return 0;
}
```

Output 1:
```
Enter a number you want to check.
25
25 is odd
```
Output 2
```
Enter a number you want to check.
2
2 is even
```

Program 3.5: Check whether a given integer number is positive or negative.
```c
#include <stdio.h>
#include <conio.h>
void main()
{
   int number;
   clrscr();
   printf("Enter a number\n");
   scanf ("%d", &number);
   if (number > 0)
      printf ("%d, is a positive number\n", number);
   else
      printf ("%d, is a negative number\n", number);
}
```
Output 1:
```
Enter a number
-5
-5, is a negative number
```
Output 2:
```
Enter a number
89
89, is a positive number
```

Program 3.6: Find whether a given year is leap year or not.
```c
#include <stdio.h>
void main()
{
   int year;
   printf("Enter a year\n");
   scanf("%d",&year);
   if ( (year % 4) == 0)
   printf("%d is a leap year",year);
   else
   printf("%d is not a leap year\n",year);
}
```

Output 1:
```
Enter a year
2000
2000 is a leap year
```
Output 2:
```
Enter a year
2007
2007 is not a leap year
```

Program 3.7: Program to add two complex numbers.

```c
#include <stdio.h>
/* We use structure for this program. For structure details see Chapter 6 */
struct complex
{
   int real, img;
};
int main()
{
   struct complex a, b, c;
   printf("Enter a and b where a + ib is the first complex number.\n");
   printf("a = ");
   scanf("%d", &a.real);
   printf("b = ");
   scanf("%d", &a.img);
   printf("Enter c and d where c + id is the second complex number.\n");
   printf("c = ");
   scanf("%d", &b.real);
   printf("d = ");
   scanf("%d", &b.img);
   c.real = a.real + b.real;
   c.img = a.img + b.img;
   if ( c.img >= 0 )
    printf("Sum of two complex numbers = %d + %di\n",c.real,c.img);
   else
    printf("Sum of two complex numbers = %d %di\n",c.real,c.img);
   return 0;
}
```

Output:
```
Enter a and b where a + ib is the first complex number.
a = 3
b = 4
Enter c and d where c + id is the second complex number.
c = 2
d = 1
Sum of two complex numbers = 5 + 5i
```

Nested if Statement:
- A nested if statement is simply an if statement within an if statement.
- The nested if statement enables us to specify multiple actions in a single instruction.
- The **syntax for a nested if** statement is as follows:
```
if( boolean_expression 1)
{
    /* Executes when the boolean expression 1 is true */
    if(boolean_expression 2)
    {
        /* Executes when the boolean expression 2 is true */
    }
}
```

Program 3.8: Program to find greatest in three numbers.
```
#include<stdio.h>
#include<conio.h>
void main()
{
    int a,b,c;
    clrscr();
    printf("\n Enter value of a, b & c: ");
    scanf("%d %d %d",&a,&b,&c);
    if((a>b)&&(a>c))
    printf("\n a is greatest");
    if((b>c)&&(b>a))
    printf("\n b is greatest");
    if((c>a)&&(c>b))
    printf("\n c is greatest");
    getch();
}
```
Output:
```
Enter value of a,b & c: 15 17 21
c is greatest
```

Program 3.9: Program for GCD and LCM of two integers.

```c
#include <stdio.h>
#include <conio.h>
void main()
{
    int num1, num2, gcd, lcm, remainder, numerator, denominator;
    clrscr();
    printf("Enter two numbers\n");
    scanf("%d %d", &num1,&num2);
    if (num1 > num2)
    {
        numerator = num1;
        denominator = num2;
    }
    else
    {
        numerator = num2;
        denominator = num1;
    }
    remainder = num1 % num2;
    while(remainder !=0)
    {
        numerator = denominator;
        denominator = remainder;
        remainder = numerator % denominator;
    }
    gcd = denominator;
    lcm = num1 * num2 / gcd;
    printf("GCD of %d and %d = %d \n", num1,num2,gcd);
    printf("LCM of %d and %d = %d \n", num1,num2,lcm);
}    /* End of main() */
```

Output:
```
Enter two numbers
5
15
GCD of 5 and 15 = 5
LCM of 5 and 15 = 15
```

3.2.3 Nested if-else Statement

- It is a conditional statement which is used when we want to check more than one conditions at a time in a same program.
- The conditions are executed from top to bottom checking each condition whether it meets the conditional criteria or not.
- If it found the condition is true then it executes the block of associated statements of true part else it goes to next condition to execute.

Syntax:
```
if(condition)
{
    if(condition)
    {
        statements;
    }
    else
    {
        statements;
    }
}
else
{
    statements;
}
```

- In above syntax, the condition is checked first. If it is true, then the program control flow goes inside the braces and again checks the next condition. If it is true then it executes the block of statements associated with it else executes else part.
- Fig. 3.6 shows flowchart for nested if-else statement.

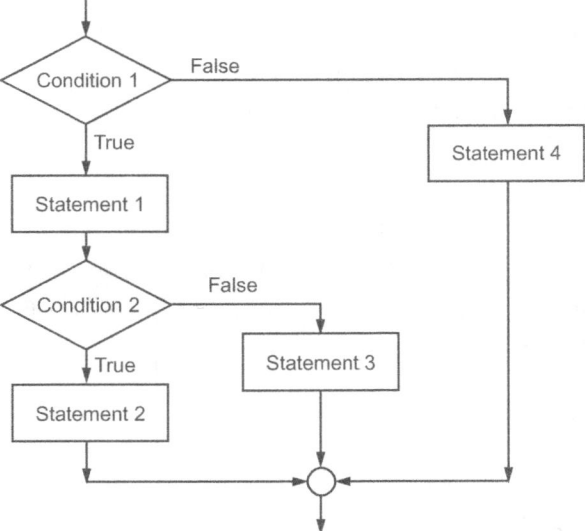

Fig. 3.6: Flowchart for nested if-else statement

Program 3.10: Program to demonstrate nested if-else statement.
```c
#include<stdio.h>
#include<conio.h>
void main()
{
    int no;
    clrscr();
    printf("\n Enter Number:");
    scanf("%d",&no);
    if(no>0)
    {
        printf("\n\n Number is greater than 0!");
    }
    else
    {
        if(no==0)
        {
        printf("\n\n It is 0!");
        }
        else
        {
        printf("Number is less than 0 !");
        }
    }
    getch();
}
```
Output 1:
```
Enter Number: 0
It is 0!
```
Output 2:
```
Enter Number: 7
Number is greater than 0!
```

else-if Ladder:
- In C programming language the else if ladder is a way of putting multiple ifs together when multipath decisions are involved. It is a one of the types of decision making and branching statements.
- A multipath decision is a chain of if's in which the statement associated with each else is an if.

- The **syntax** of else if ladder is as follows:
```
if (condition_1)
{
   statement_1;
}
 else if (condition_2)
 {
   statement_2;
   }
    else if (condition_n)
  {
   statement_n;
   }
   else
  {
   default statment;
       }
 statement-x;
```
- Above construct is known as the else if ladder. The conditions are evaluated from the top of the ladder to downwards.
- As soon as a true condition is found, the statement associated with it is executed and the control is transferred to the statement-x (skipping the rest of the ladder). When all the n conditions become false, then the final else containing the default statement will be executed.
- Fig. 3.7 shows flowchart for if-else ladder.

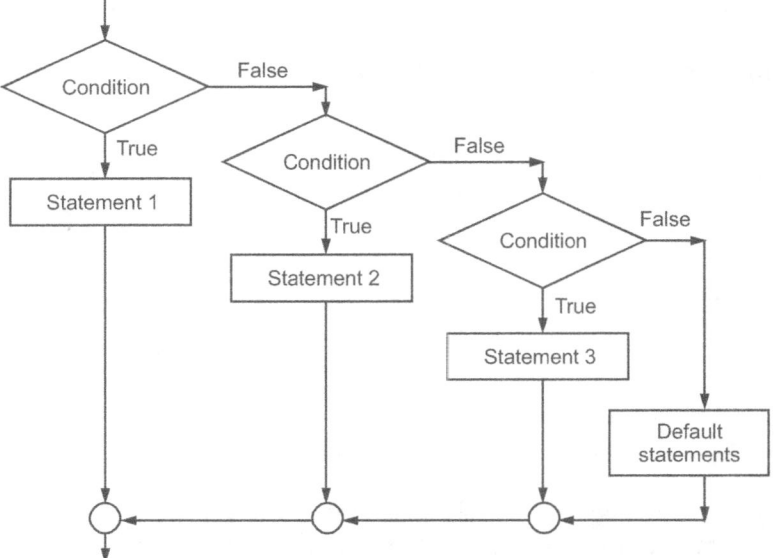

Fig. 3.7: Flowchart for if-else ladder

- Below is the sample C program of the if – else ladder statement in which the color is to be selected by using the if – else ladder.

Program 3.11: Program to demonstrate else_if ladder.
```c
#include<stdio.h>
#include<string.h>
void main()
{
    int n;
    printf(" Enter 1 to 4 to select random color");
    scanf("%d",&n);
    if(n==1)
    {
        printf("You selected Red color");
    }
    else if(n==2)
    {
        printf("You selected Green color");
    }
    else if(n==3)
    {
        printf("You selected yellow color");
    }
    else if(n==4)
    {
        printf("You selected Blue color");
    }
        else
    {
        printf("No color selected");
    }
    getch();
}
```
Output:
```
Enter 1 to 4 to select random color 3
You selected yellow color
```

Program 3.12: Program to accept marks and print the grade.

```c
#include<stdio.h>
void main()
{
    int a, b, c, d, e, per;
    clrscr();
    printf("Enter marks of four subject:");
    scanf("%d %d %d %d", &a, &b, &c, &d);
    if(a < 40 || b < 40 || c < 40 || d < 40)
    printf("\n You have failed in one subject");
    per = (a + b + c + d)/4;
    if (per >= 60)
    printf("\n First class");
    else
    {
        if(per <=59 && per >=55)
        printf("\n Higher second class");
        else if(per <=54 && per >= 40)
            printf("Second class");
        else
            printf("\n Fail");
    }
    getch();
}
```

Output:
```
Enter marks of four subject : 35  65  87  48
You have failed in one subject
Higher second class
```

3.2.4 switch Statement

- Switch statement is a multiple or multiway branding decision making statement.
- When we use nested if-else statement to check more than one conditions then the complexity of a program increases in case of a lot of conditions. Thus, the program is difficult to read and maintain. So to overcome this problem, C provides 'switch statement'.
- Switch statememt checks the value of a expression against a case values, if condition matches the case values then the control is transferred to that point.

Syntax:
```
switch(expression)
{
    case expr1:
        statements;
        break;
    case expr2:
        statements;
        break;
    case exprn:
        statements;
        break;
    default:
        statements;
}
```

- In above syntax, switch, case, break are keywords. expr1, expr2 are known as 'case labels.' Statements inside case expression need not to be closed in braces. Break statement causes an exit from switch statement. Default case is optional case. When neither any match found, it executes.
- Fig. 3.8 shows flowchart of switch statement.

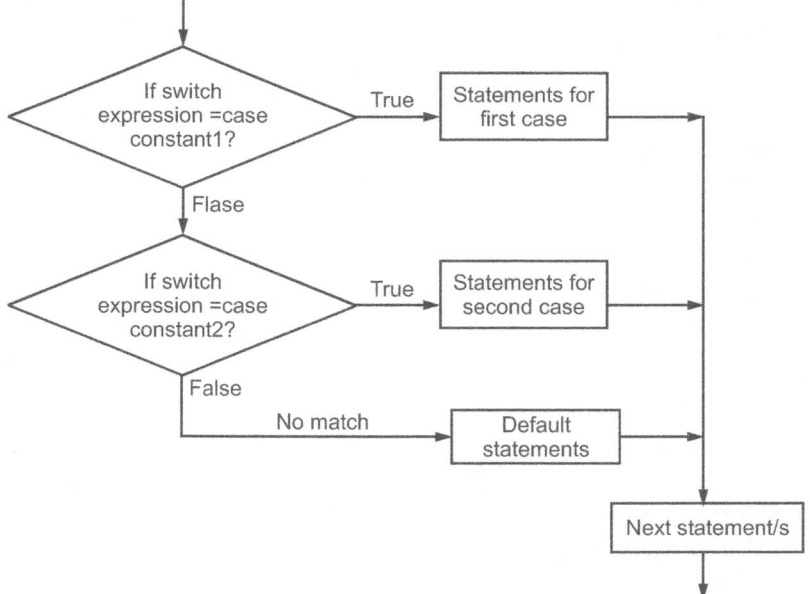

Fig. 3.8: Flowchart of switch...case statement

- Rules for declaring switch case statement:
  1. Case labels must end with (:) colon.
  2. The case label should be integer or character constant.
  3. Each compound statement of a switch case should contain break statement to exit from case.

Program 3.13: Write a program to demonstrate switch statement.

```
/*switch statement demonstration*/
#include<stdio.h>
#include<conio.h>
void main()
 {
   int color = 1;
   printf("Please choose a color \n");
   printf("1: red\t\t2: green\t\t3: blue:\n");
   scanf("%d", &color);
   switch (color)
   {
      case 1:
         printf("you chose red color\n");
         break;
      case 2:
         printf("you chose green color\n");
         break;
      case 3:
         printf("you chose blue color\n");
         break;
      default:
         printf("you did not choose any color\n");
   }
   getch();
 }
```

Output:
```
Please choose a color
1: red      2: green      3: blue:
2
you chose green color
```

Program 3.14: Program to find greater number using switch statement.

```c
#include<stdio.h>
#include<conio.h>
void main()
{
    int number;
    clrscr();
    printf("Enter a number \n");
    scanf("%d",&number);
    switch(number)
    {
        case 1:
            printf("Given number is 1\n");
            break;
        case 2:
            printf("Given number is 2\n");
            break;
        case 3:
            printf("Given number is 3\n");
            break;
        case 4:
            printf("Given number is 4\n");
            break;
        case 5:
            printf("Given number is 5\n");
            break;
        default:
            {
            if(number<0)
                printf("Given number is negative");
            else
                printf("Given number is greater than 5");
            }
    }
    getch();
}
```

Output 1:
```
Enter a number
10
Given number is greater than 5
```
Output 2:
```
Enter a number
3
Given number is 3
```

Program 3.15: Program to check entered character is vowel or not.
```c
/*check vowel or not using switch*/
#include<stdio.h>
#include<conio.h>
void main()
{
  char ch;
  clrscr();
  printf("Enter a character\n");
  scanf("%c", &ch);
  switch(ch)
  {
    case 'a':
    case 'A':
    case 'e':
    case 'E':
    case 'i':
    case 'I':
    case 'o':
    case 'O':
    case 'u':
    case 'U':
      printf("%c is a vowel.\n", ch);
      break;
    default:
      printf("%c is not a vowel.\n", ch);
  }
  getch();
}
```
Output:
```
Enter a character
R
R is not a vowel.
```

Program 3.16: Program to Input a direction code and print the direction name.

```c
#include<stdio.h>
#include<conio.h>
void main()
{
char y;
clrscr();
printf("\n Enter the code :\t");
scanf("%c",&y);
switch (y)
{
   case 'N' : printf("\n North Direction");
            break;
   case 'S' : printf("\n South Direction");
            break;
   case 'E' : printf("\n East Direction");
            break;
   default :  printf("\n West Direction");
            break;
}
getch();
}
```

Output:
```
Enter the code : S
South Direction
```

Program 3.17: Program to accept month and print the season.

```c
#include<conio.h>
#include<stdio.h>
void main(void)
{
  int month;
  printf("\n Enter month: ");
  scanf("%d", &month);
```

```
        switch (month)
        {
           case 12:
           case 1:
           case 2:
                   printf("\n month %d is a winter season.", month);
                   break;
           case 3:
           case 4:
           case 5:
                   printf("\n month %d is a spring season.", month);
                   break;
           case 6:
           case 7:
           case 8:
                   printf("\n month %d is a summer season.", month);
                   break;
           case 9:
           case 10:
           case 11:
                   printf("\n month %d is a fall season.", month);
                   break;
           default:
                   printf("\n month %d is not a valid month\n", month);
        }
        getch();
    }
```

Output:
```
    Enter month: 9
    month 9 is a fall season
```

Program 3.18: Program to print the days of week.
```
    #include<stdio.h>
    #include<conio.h>
    void main( )
       {
       int day;
       clrscr( );
       printf("\nEnter day of week as numbers from 1 to 7\t");
       scanf("%d",&day);
```

```
        switch(day)
        {
            case 1:
                printf("\nMonday");
                break;
            case 2:
                printf("\nTuesday");
                break;
            case 3:
                printf("\nWednesday");
                break;
            case 4:
                printf("\nThursday");
                break;
            case 5:
                printf("\nFriday");
                break;
            case 6:
                printf("\nSaturday");
                break;
            case 7:
                printf("\nSunday");
                break;
            default:
                printf("Wrong Input");
            getch( );
        }
```
Output:
```
Enter day of work as number from 1 to 7 5
Friday
```

Advantages of switch case statement:
1. Complexity of a program is minimized.
2. Easy and simple to use and understand.
3. Easy to find out errors.

Nested Switch Statement:
- Switch in a switch is called nested switch.
- The syntax for a **nested switch** statement is as follows:
```
switch(ch1) {
   case 'A':
      printf("This A is part of outer switch" );
      switch(ch2) {
   case 'A':
      printf("This A is part of inner switch" );
      break;
   case 'B': /* case code */
}
break;
case 'B': /* case code */
}
```

Program 3.19: Program for nested switch statement.
```
#include <stdio.h>
int main ()
{
 /* local variable definition */
 int a = 100;
 int b = 200;
 switch(a)
{
 case 100:
 printf("This is part of outer switch\n", a );
 switch(b)
{
 case 200:
 printf("This is part of inner switch\n", a );
 }
 }
 printf("Exact value of a is: %d\n", a );
 printf("Exact value of b is: %d\n", b );
 return 0;
}
```
Output:
```
This is part of outer switch
This is part of inner switch
Exact value of a is: 100
Exact value of b is: 200
```

Difference between if-else and switch statements:

if-else Statement	switch Statement

1. This statement allows only two way branching from a single expression. As shown below:
 	
if-else (exp.) — True → Statement 1
              — False → Statement 2
	1. This statement allows multiway branching from as single expression. As shown below:
	
	switch (exp.) — case value 1
	             — case value 2
	             — case value 3
	             — case value 4.
	                .
	                .
	             — default

2. Putting { and } braces is essential.	2. switch statement belonging to a case need not be need { and } braces.
3. Tracing of errors and debugging is expensive and difficult.	3. Tracing of errors and debugging is easy.
4. This statement is in elegant and complicated to write.	4. This statement is very elegant and easier to write.
5. Using this statement code/program become complex.	5. Code became simple and easy.

6. **Syntax:**
`if condition`
`{`
    `statements ...`
`}`
    `else`
    `{`
        `statements ...`
    `}`
	6. **Syntax:**
	`switch (variable)`
	`{`
	`case value 1:`
	`break;`
	`case value 2:`
	`break;`
	`:`
	`default:`
	`}`

3.2.5 Conditional Operator

- This is the only ternary operator in C language. It is denoted by?: symbol.
- Conditional operator (?:) has the following general form:
    Exp1? Exp2: Exp3;
    Where, Exp1, Exp2, and Exp3 are expressions.
- The value of a ? expression is determined like this: Exp1 is evaluated. If it is true, then Exp2 is evaluated and becomes the value of the entire ? expression. If Exp1 is false, then Exp3 is evaluated and its value becomes the value of the expression.

Program 3.20: Check whether number is Odd or Even using conditional operators.

```c
#include<stdio.h>
int main()
{
   int num, flag;
   printf("Enter the Number: ");
   scanf("%d",&num);
      flag = ((num%2==0)?0:1);
   if(flag==0)
    printf("\nEven");
   else
    printf("\nOdd");
    return(0);
}
```

Output 1:
   Enter the Number: 4
   Even

Output 2:
   Enter the Number: 3
   Odd

3.3 Loops

- Iterative statements are used to run a particular block statements repeatedly or in other words from a loop.
- A loop is a part of code of a program which is executed repeatedly.
- A loop is used using condition. The repetition is done until condition becomes condition true.
- A loop declaration and execution can be done in following ways.
   o Check condition to start a loop
   o Initialize loop with declaring a variable.
   o Executing statements inside loop.
   o Increment or decrement of value of a variable.
- **Types of looping statements:** Basically, the types of looping statements depends on the condition checking mode. Condition checking can be made in two ways as: Before loop and after loop. So, there are 2 (two) types of looping statements.
   1. **Entry controlled loop:** In such type of loop, the test condition is checked first before the loop is executed. Some common examples of this looping statements are while loop and for loop.

2. **Exit controlled loop:** In such type of loop, the loop is executed first. Then condition is checked after block of statements are executed. The loop executed atleast one time compulsorily. Common example of this looping statement is a do-while loop.

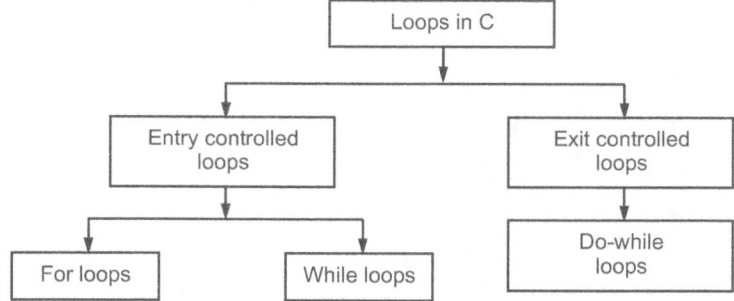

Fig. 3.9 (a): Loop is C language

3.3.1 for Loop

- This is an entry controlled looping statement.
- In for loop structure, more than one variable can be initilized.
- One of the most important feature of this loop is that the three actions can be taken at a time like variable initilization, condition checking and increment/decrement.
- The for loop can be more concise and flexible than that of while and do-while loops.

    Syntax:
    ```
    for(initialization; test-condition; increment/decrement)
    {
        statements;
    }
    ```
- In above syntax, the given three expressions are seperated by ; (Semicolon).

How for loop works in C programming?

- The initial expression is initialized only once at the beginning of the for loop. Then, the test expression is checked by the program. If the test expression is false, for loop is terminated.
- But, if test expression is true then, the codes are executed and update expression is updated. Again, the test expression is checked. If it is false, loop is terminated and if it is true, the same process repeats until test expression is false. Fig. 3.9 (b) shows flowchart for the working of for loop in C programming.

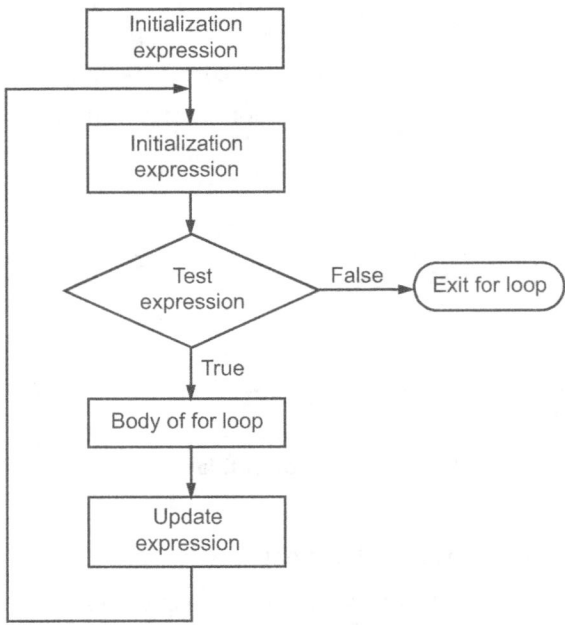

Fig. 3.9 (b): Flowchart of for loop

- **Features of for loop:**
    1. More concise,
    2. Easy to use,
    3. Highly flexible,
    4. More than one variable can be initialized,
    5. More than one increments can be applied, and
    6. More than two conditions can be used.

Program 3.21: Program for 'for' loop.
```
#include<stdio.h>
#include<conio.h>
void main()
{
    int a i;
    clrscr();
    for(i=0; i<5; i++)
    {
        printf("\n\t Nirali prakashan"); // 5 times
    }
    getch();
}
```

Output:
```
Nirali prakashan
Nirali prakashan
Nirali prakashan
Nirali prakashan
Nirali prakashan
```

Program 3.22: Program to print fibonacci series. The first two Fibonacci numbers are 0 and 1 then next number is addition of previous two numbers.

0, 1, 1, 2, 3, 5, 8, 13, 21, 34, 55, 89.....

In mathematics it is defined by recurrence relation.

```c
#include<stdio.h>
#include<conio.h>
void main()
{
    int a,b,c,i,n;
    clrscr();
    a=0;
    b=1;
    printf("\n enter number for how many times generate series");
    scanf("%d",&n);
    printf("\n FIBONACCI SERIES\n");
    printf("\t%d\t%d",a,b);
    for(i=0;i<n;i++)
    {
        c=a+b;
        a=b;
        b=c;
        printf("\t%d",c);
    }
    getch();
}
```

Output:
```
enter number for how many times generate series 6
FIBONACCI SERIES:
0     1     1     2     3     5     8     13
```

Program 3.23: Program to Find Factorial of a number. For any positive number n, its factorial is given by: factorial = 1*2*3*4....n and if a number is negative, factorial does not exist and factorial of 0 is 1.

```c
#include <stdio.h>
int main()
{
    int n, count;
    unsigned long long int factorial=1;
    printf("Enter an integer: ");
    scanf("%d",&n);
    if ( n< 0)
    printf("Error!!! Factorial of negative number doesn't exist.");
    else
    {
       for(count=1;count<=n;++count) /*  for   loop    terminates    if count>n */
       {
       factorial*=count; /* factorial=factorial*count */
       }
       printf("Factorial = %lu",factorial);
    }
    return 0;
}
```

Output:
```
Enter an integer: 10
Factorial = 3628800
```

Program 3.24: Program to check whether a number is prime or not.

A positive integer which is only divisible by 1 and iself is known as prime number. For example, 13 is a prime number because it is only divisible by 1 and 13 but, 15 is not prime number because it is divisible by 1, 3, 5 and 15.

```c
#include <stdio.h>
int main()
{
    int n, i, flag=0;
    printf("Enter a positive integer: ");
    scanf("%d",&n);
```

```
        for(i=2;i<=n/2;++i)
        {
           if(n%i==0)
           {
              flag=1;
              break;
           }
        }
        if (flag==0)
           printf("%d is a prime number.",n);
        else
           printf("%d is not a prime number.",n);
        return 0;
    }
```
Output

```
    Enter a positive integer: 29
    29 is a prime number.
```

Program 3.25: Program to accept a number from user then print the sum of all even numbers from 1 to n and average of number from 1 to n.

```
    #include<stdio.h>
    #include<conio.h>
    void main()
    {
        int  n, i, sum=0;
        float avg;
        clrscr();
        printf("\n Enter a number:");
        scanf("%d", &n);
        for(i=1; i<=n; i++)
        if (i%2==0)
        {
         sum=sum+i;
        }
        avg=sum/n;
        printf("\nsum  of number is %d", sum);
        printf("\naverage  is %f", avg);
        getch();
    }
```
Output:

```
    Enter a number 15
    sum of number is 56
    average is 3.00
```

Program 3.26: Program to accept a number from user that is n then print all the odd number from n to 1.

```c
#include<stdio.h>
#include<conio.h>
void main()
{
    int  n,i;
    clrscr();
    printf("\n Enter any odd number : ");
    scanf("%d", &n);
    for (i=n; i>=1; i--)
    {
    printf("\t%d", i);
    i=i-1;
    }
    getch();
}
```

Output:

Enter a number : 21
21 19 17 15 13 11 9 7 5 3

Nested for Loop:

- One for loop can be nested within another for loop.
- **Syntax:**

```
for (initializing; test condition; increment/decrement)
{
statement;
for (initializing; test condition; increment/decrement)
{
body of inner loop;
}
statement;
}
```

Program 3.27: Program to print "Hello !".
```
#include<stdio.h>
void main()
{
   int i, j;
   for(i=1;i<=3;i++) /* Outer for Loop */
   {
      for(j=1;j<=2;j++)    /* Inner for Loop */
      {
         printf("Hello!\n");
      }
   }
}
```
Output:
```
Hello!
Hello!
Hello!
Hello!
Hello!
Hello!
```

- Here, there are two for loops. The first (outer) for loop has condition i<=3 and the second (inner) for loop has condition i<=2. The inner for loop will get executed completely for every iteration of the outer for loop.

Hence, when
$$\left.\begin{array}{l} i = 1 \quad j = 1 \;,\; j = 2 \\ i = 2 \quad j = 1 \;,\; j = 2 \\ i = 3 \quad j = 1 \;,\; j = 2 \end{array}\right\}$$ in all there will be 3 × 2 = 6 iterations

Thus, 'Hello' will get displayed 6 times.

Program 3.28: Program to print:
```
* * * *
* * * *
* * * *
* * * *
```

```
#include<stdio.h>
void main()
{
int i, j;
clrscr();
for (j=1; j<=4; j++)
{
printf("\n");
```

```
for (i=1; i<=4; i++)
{
printf("*");
}
getch();
}
```

Output:
```
* * * *
* * * *
* * * *
* * * *
```

Program 3.29: Program to print the rectangle pyramid of numbers.
```
1 1 1 1 1
2 2 2 2 2
3 3 3 3 3
4 4 4 4 4
5 5 5 5 5
#include<stdio.h>
int main()
{
int number,row,col;
printf("\n Enter Number of Rows to be display: ");
scanf("%d",&number);
for(row=1; number>=row; row++)
{
for(col=1; col <= number; col++)
printf("%d",row);
printf("\n");
}
return 0;
}
```

Output:
```
Enter Number of Rows to be display: 5
1 1 1 1 1
2 2 2 2 2
3 3 3 3 3
4 4 4 4 4
5 5 5 5 5
```

Program 3.30: Print following right angled binary pyramid in C programming.
```
1
0 1
1 0 1
0 1 0 1
1 0 1 0 1
```
```c
#include <stdio.h>
int main(void)
{
int i, j;
for (i = 0; i < 5; i++)
{
for (j = 0; j <= i; j++)
{
if (((i + j) % 2) == 0)
{
printf("1");
}
else {
printf("\0");
}
printf("\t");
}
printf("\n");
}
return 0;
}
```
Output:
```
1
0 1
1 0 1
0 1 0 1
1 0 1 0 1
```

Program 3.31: Program to Print FLOYD triangle as given below:
```
1
2 3
4 5 6
7 8 9 10
```
```c
#include<stdio.h>
int main()
{
int i,j,k=1;
  int range;
printf("Enter the range: ");
  scanf("%d",&range);
printf("FLOYD'S TRIANGLE: \n\n");
for(i=1;i<=range;i++)
  {
  for(j=1;j<=i;j++,k++)
  printf("%d",k);
  printf("\n");
  }
return 0;
}
```
Output:
```
Enter the range: 4
FLOYD'S TRIANGLE:
1
2 3
4 5 6
7 8 9 10
```

Program 3.32: Program to print number pyramid pattern.
```c
#include<stdio.h>
#include<conio.h>
void main()
{
  int i,j;
  int num;
  clrscr();
  printf("\n Enter the number of Digits:");
  scanf("%d",&num);
```

```
    for(i=0;i<=num;i++)
    {
    for(j=0;j<i;j++)
    printf("%d ",i);
    printf("\n");
    }
    getch();
    }
```
Output:
```
    Enter the number of Digits: 4
    1
    2 2
    3 3 3
    4 4 4 4
```

Program 3.33: Program to print inverted pyramid as shown below:
```
    * * * *
    * * *
    * *
    *
```
```
    #include<stdio.h>
    #include<conio.h>
    void main()
    {
    int i,j;
    char ch = '*';
    clrscr();
    for(i=4;i>=0;i--)
    {
    printf("\n");
     for(j=0;j<i;j++)
     printf("%c",ch);
    }
    getch();
    }
```

Program 3.34: Print this right angled pyramid in c using nested loops.

```
*
* *
* * *
* * * *
* * * * *
* * * * * *
```

```c
#include<stdio.h>
#include<conio.h>
main()
{
int i,j,lines;
char ch = '*';
clrscr();
printf("Enter number of lines: ");
scanf("%d",&lines);
for(i=0;i <=lines;i++)
 {
 printf("\n");
 for (j=0;j < i;j++)
 printf("%c",ch);
 }
getch();
}
```

Output:
```
Enter number of lines: 6
*
* *
* * *
* * * *
* * * * *
* * * * * *
```

Program 3.35: Program to print 1-10 numbers in pyramid fashion.
```
1
2   3
4   5   6
7   8   9   10
```
Program
```c
#include<stdio.h>
#include<conio.h>
 void main()
 {
 int i,j;
 int count=1;
 for(i=0;i<=4;i++)
 {
 printf("\n");
 for(j=0;j<i;j++)
 {
 printf("%d\t",count);
 count++;
 }
 }
 getch();
 }
```
Output:
```
1
2 3
4 5 6
7 8 9 10
```

Program 3.36: Program to print pyramid of multiplication tables.
```
0
0   1
0   2   4
0   3   6   9
0   4   8   12  16
0   5   10  15  20  25
0   6   12  18  24  30  36
```

Program
```
#include<stdio.h>
void main()
{
int i,j;
clrscr();
 for(i=0;i<=6;i++)
 {
 for(j=0;j<=i;j++)
 {
 printf("%d\t",i*j);
 }
 printf("\n");
 }
 getch();
 }
```
Output:
```
0
0  1
0  2   4
0  3   6   9
0  4   8   12  16
0  5   10  15  20  25
0  6   12  18  24  30  36
```

3.3.2 while Loop

- This is an entry controlled looping statement. It is used to repeat a block of statements until condition becomes true.

   Syntax:
   ```
   while(condition)
   {
       statements;
       increment/decrement;
   }
   ```

- In above syntax, the condition is checked first. If it is true, then the program control flow goes inside the loop and executes the block of statements associated with it. At the end of loop increment or decrement is done to change in variable value. This process continues until test condition satisfies.

- In the beginning of while loop, test expression is checked. If it is true, codes inside the body of while loop, i.e, code/s inside parentheses are executed and again the test expression is checked and process continues until the test expression becomes false.
- Fig. 3.10 shows flowchart fore while loop.

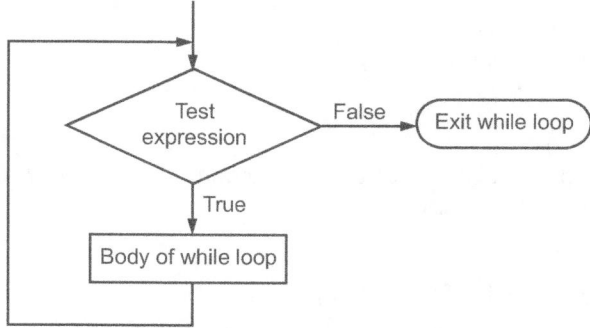

Fig. 3.10: Flowchart of while loop

Program 3.37: Program for while loop.

```
#include<stdio.h>
#include<conio.h>
void main()
{
    int a;
    clrscr();
    a=1;
    while(a<=5)
    {
        printf("\n Nirali Prakashan");
        a+=1; /* i.e. a = a + 1 */
    }
    getch();
}
```

Output:

```
Nirali Prakashan
Nirali Prakashan
Nirali Prakashan
Nirali Prakashan
Nirali Prakashan
```

Program 3.38: Program to find the factorial of a number, where the number is entered by user. (Hints: factorial of n = 1*2*3*...*n).

```
#include <stdio.h>
 int main()
{
 int number,factorial;
 printf("Enter a number.\n");
 scanf("%d",&number);
 factorial=1;
 while (number>0)
{ /* while loop continues util test condition number>0 is true */
 factorial=factorial*number;
 --number;
}
printf("Factorial=%d",factorial);
return 0;
}
```

Output
```
Enter a number.
6
Factorial=720
```

Nested while loop:

- **Syntax** for nested while loop is
```
while(condition 1)
{
   statement 1;
   while (condition 2)
   statement 2;
}
```

Program 3.39: Program to print the number from 1 to 10 using a 'while' loop.
```
#include<stdio.h>
#include<conio.h>
void main()
{
int num = 1;                /* initialize counter */
while(num<=10)              /* check the condition */
   {                        /* start of loop */
      printf("\t%d",num);   /* print the number */
      num++;                /* increment the counter */
   }                        /* end of loop */
getch();
}
```
Output:
```
  1  2  3  4  5  6  7  8  9  10
```

Program 3.40: Program to print the addition of all the numbers from 10 to 20 using a 'while' loop.

```
#include<stdio.h>
#include<conio.h>
void main()
{
int x = 10, sum = 0;           /* initialize variables */
while(x <=20)                  /* check the condition */
    {                          /* start of the loop */
        sum = sum + x;         /* add the values */
        x++;                   /* increment counter */
    }                          /* end of the loop */
printf("\nAddition is : %d",sum);  /* print addition */
getch();
}
```

Output:
```
Addition is : 165
```

Program 3.41: Program to find entered number is prime or not.

```
#include<stdio.h>
#include<conio.h>
void main()
{
    int num,i,count=0;
    printf("Enter a number: ");
    scanf("%d",&num);
    i=2;
    while(i<=num/2)
    {
       if(num%i==0)
       {
          count++;
          break;
       }
    } i++;
    if(count==0 && num!= 1)
        printf("%d is a prime number",num);
    else
        printf("%d is not a prime number",num);
    getch();
}
```

Output:
```
Enter a number: 5
5 is a prime number
```

Program 3.42: Program to print Fibonacci series up to the number entered by user.

```c
/*print Fibonacci series*/
#include<stdio.h>
#include<conio.h>
void main()
{
int a=0,b=1,c,i=2,n;
clrscr();
printf("\n Enter number : ");
scanf("%d",&n);
if(n==0)
printf("%d,a);
else
printf("%d %d",a,b);
while(i<=n)
  {
    c=a+b;
    printf("\t%d",c);
    a=b;
    b=c;
    i++;
  }
getch();
}
```

Output 1:

Enter number : 5

0 1 1 2 3 5

Output 2:

Enter number : 8

0 1 1 2 3 5 8 13 21

Program 3.43: Program to print the digits in reverse order.

```c
/*print the digits in reverse order*/
#include <stdio.h>
#include <conio.h>
void main()
{
  int n,j;
  clrscr();
  printf("Enter the No :- ");
  scanf("%d",&n);
  printf("\n");
  printf("Reverce of the number is....");
  while(n>0)
    {
        j = n%10;
        printf("%d",j);
        n= n/10;
    }
  getch();
}
```

Output:

```
Enter the No :- 23456
Reverce of the number is....65432
```

3.3.3 do-while Loop

- This is an exit controlled looping statement.
- Sometimes, there is need to execute a block of statements first then to check condition. At that time such type of a loop is used.
- In do_while, block of statements are executed first and then condition is checked.

Syntax:
```
do
{
   statements;
   (increment/decrement);
} while(condition);
```

- In above syntax, the first the block of statements are executed. At the end of loop, while statement is executed. If the resultant condition is true then program control goes to evaluate the body of a loop once again. This process continues till condition becomes true. When it becomes false, then the loop terminates.
- At first codes inside body of do is executed. Then, the test expression is checked. If it is true, code/s inside body of do are executed again and the process continues until test expression becomes false(zero). Notice, there is semicolon in the end of while (); in do...while loop.
- Fig. 3.11 shows flowchart of do-while loop.

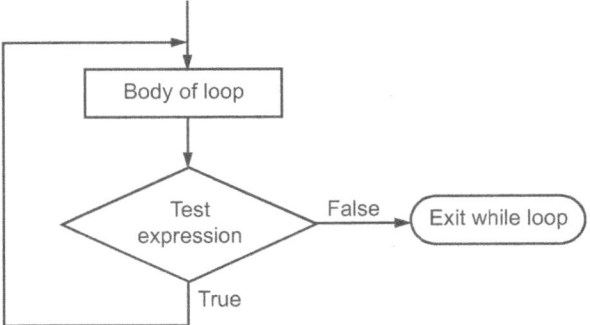

Fig. 3.11: Flowchart of do...while loop

Note: The while statement should be terminated with ; (semicolon).

Program 3.44: Program for do-while loop.

```
#include<stdio.h>
#include<conio.h>
void main()
{
   int a;
   clrscr();
   a=1;
   do
   {
      printf("\n\t Nirali Prakashan");  // 5 times
      a+=1;    // i.e. a = a + 1
   }while(a<=5);
   a=6;
   do
   {
      printf("\n\n\t Pragati");   // 1 time
      a+=1;    // i.e. a = a + 1
   }while(a<=5);
   getch();
}
```

Output:
```
Nirali prakashan
Nirali prakashan
Nirali prakashan
Nirali prakashan
Nirali prakashan
Pragati
```

Comparison between while and do-while loops:

Sr. No.	while loop	do-while loop
1.	It checks the condition at the start of the loop	It checks the condition at the end of the loop
2.	This is of type entry controlled loop structure	This is of type exit controlled loop structure
3.	The while loop is called as pre-test loop	The do-while loop is called as post-test loop
4.	It is not guaranteed that how many times the loop body will get executed.	The loop body will be executed at least once.

5.	**Syntax:**
	while(condition)
	{
	//loop body
	}
		Syntax:
		do
		{
		//loop body
		}while(condition);

3.4 Jump Statements

- Jump statements are used to make the flow of your statements from one point to another.

3.4.1 goto Statement

- It is a well known as 'jumping statement.'
- The goto statement is used to change the normal sequence of program execution by transferring control to other part of the program.
- The general format is,
    ```
    goto label:
    ```
    where label is an identifier to label the target statement to which the control will be transferred. The target must be labelled and the label must be followed by a colon.
- So the general format of target statement is:
    ```
    label: statements;
    ```

- It is primarily used to transfer the control of execution to any place in a program. It is useful to provide branching within a loop.
- When the loops are deeply nested at that if an error occurs then it is difficult to get exited from such loops. Simple break statement cannot work here properly. In this situations, goto statement is used.
- Fig. 3.12 shows working of goto statement.

Fig. 3.12: Working of goto statement

Program 3.45: Program for goto statement.

```
#include<stdio.h>
#include<conio.h>
void main()
{
    int i=1, j;
    clrscr();
    while(i<=3)
    {
        for(j=1; j<=3; j++)
        {
            printf(" * ");
            if(j==2)
            goto stop;
        }
        i = i + 1;
    }
    stop:
        printf("\n\n Exited !");
    getch();
}
```

Output:
```
* *

Exited!
```

Labelled Statements:

- Any statement with a label attached to it can be referred to as a labelled statement.
- Labelled statement are used as targets/way points for jump and selection statement.
- The labelled statement are represented as:

    <label>:statements;

- Label points to the statement to executed next.

3.4.2 break Statement

- Sometimes, it is necessary to exit immediately from a loop as soon as the condition is satisfied.
- When break statement is used inside a loop, then it can cause to terminate from a loop. The statements after break statement are skipped.

    Syntax:

    break;

- Fig. 3.13 show flowchart for break statement.

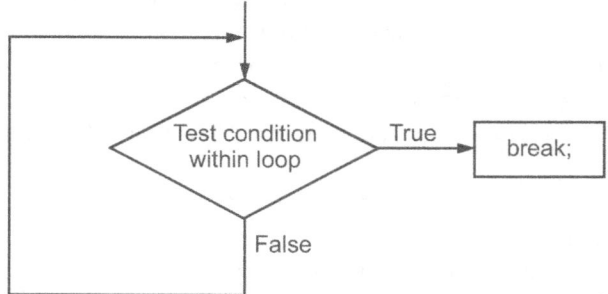

Fig. 3.13: Flowchart of break statement

Fig. 3.14 below explains the working of break statement in all three type of loops.

Fig. 3.14: Working of break statement in different loops

Program 3.46: Program for break statement.

```c
#include<stdio.h>
#include<conio.h>
void main()
{
    int i;
    clrscr();
    for(i=1; ; i++)
    {
        if(i>5)
        break;
        printf("%d",i); // 5 times only
    }
    getch();
}
```

Output:
```
1 2 3 4 5
```

3.4.3 continue Statement

- Sometimes, it is required to skip a part of a body of loop under specific conditions. So, C supports 'continue' statement to overcome this anomaly.
- The working structure of 'continue' is similar as that of that break statement but difference is that it cannot terminate the loop.
- It causes the loop to be continued with next iteration after skipping statements in between.
- Continue statement simply skipps statements and continues next iteration.
- **Syntax:** continue;
- Just like break, continue is also used with conditional if statement.
- Fig. 3.15 shows flowchart for continue statement.

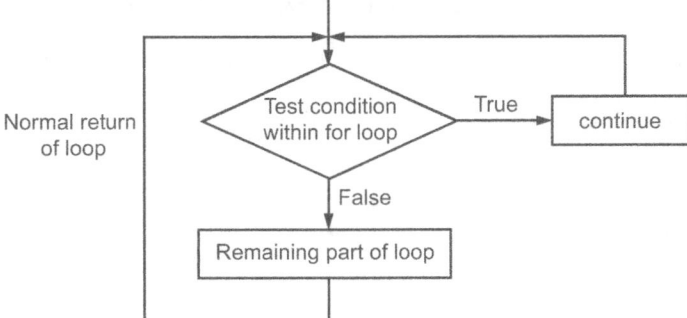

Fig. 3.15: Flowchart of continue statement

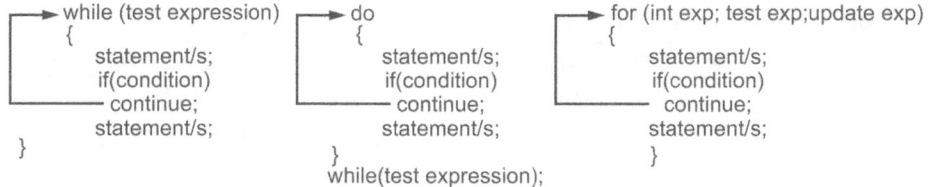

Fig. 3.16: Working of continue statement in different loops

Program 3.47: Program to demonstrate continue statement.

```
#include<stdio.h>
#include<conio.h>
void main()
{
    int i;
    clrscr();
    for(i=1; i<=10; i++)
    {
        if(i==6)
        continue;
        printf("\n\t %d",i); // 6 is omitted
    }
    getch();
}
```

Output:
```
    1
    2
    3
    4
    5
    7
    8
    9
    10
```

Comparison between break and continue statements:

Sr. No.	break Statement	continue Statement
1.	break statement causes loop termination.	continue statement does not causes loop termination.

2.	**Syntax:**
	    break;
		Syntax:
		    continue;

3.	break statement takes control to the first statement outside the control statement.	continue statement takes control to the beginning of the loop.
4.	It is used in switch and loops statements.	It is only used in loop.

5.	Example:
	    init i = 4;
	    while(i)
	    {
	        i—;
	        if (i = = 2)
	        break;
	        printf ("%d", i);}
	    }
		Example:
		    init i = 4;
		    while(i)
		    {
		        i—;
		        if (i = = 2)
		        continue;
		        printf ("%d", i);}
		    }

3.4.4 exit() Function

- The exit() function terminates the program totally. Such forced program termination is required when an error condition is detected by the program.
- As we know the program is automatically terminated when the last statement in the main() function is executed. But, to forcefully terminate the program, the exit() function is employed.

Syntax:
    exit (n);
The parameter n is an integer value, which decides the exit status.

- We can use the exit() function without 'n' also as,
    exit ( );
- In such cases, the value of n is considered as 0 by default. Any non-zero of n stands for different error conditions in program.

Program 3.48: Program to print the following pattern.
    1
    1 2
    1 2 3
    1 2 3 4

```c
#include<stdio.h>
#include<conio.h>
```

```
void main()
{
    int number = 1, n, c, k;
    printf("Enter number of rows\n");
    scanf("%d",&n);
    for ( c = 1 ; c <= n ; c++ )
    {
        for( k = 1 ; k <= c ; k++ )
        {
            printf("%d ", number);
            number++;
        }
        number = 1;
        printf("\n");
    }
    getch();
}
```
Output:
```
Enter number of rows
4
1
1 2
1 2 3
1 2 3 4
```

Program 3.49: Program to print the following pattern.
```
   *
  * *
 * * *
* * * *
```
```
#include<stdio.h>
#include<conio.h>
void main()
{
    int n, c, k = 2, j;
    printf("Enter number of rows\n");
    scanf("%d",&n);
```

```
        for ( j = 1 ; j <= n ; j++ )
        {
           for ( c = 1 ; c <= 2*n-k ; c++)
           {
              printf(" ");
           }
        k = k + 2;
        for ( c = 1 ; c <= j ; c++)
        {
           printf("*   ");
        }
           printf("\n");
        }
        getch();
    }
```

Output:
```
Enter number of rows 4
         *
       *   *
     *   *   *
   *   *   *   *
```

Program 3.50: Program to print the following pattern.

```
            1
          1 2 1
        1 2 3 2 1
      1 2 3 4 3 2 1
    1 2 3 4 5 4 3 2 1
```
```
#include <stdio.h>
#include<conio.h>
void main()
{
int  i, j, k, l;
clrscr();
for (i=1; i<=5; i++)
{
for (k=1; k<=5-i; k++)
{
printf("%d", (" ");
}
```

```c
        for (j=1; j<=i; j++)
        {
        printf("%d", j);
        }
        for(i=i-1; i>=1; i--)
        {
        printf("%d", i);
        }
        printf("\n");
        }
        getch();
        }
```

- **Program 3.51:** C programming code to check whether a number is armstrong or not. A number is armstrong if the sum of cubes of individual digits of a number is equal to the number itself. For example 371 is an armstrong number as $3^3 + 7^3 + 1^3 = 371$. Some other armstrong numbers are: 0, 1, 153, 370, 407.

```c
#include <stdio.h>
int main()
{
  int number, sum = 0, temp, remainder;
printf("Enter an integer\n");
  scanf("%d",&number);
  temp = number;
  while( temp != 0 )
  {
  remainder = temp%10;
  sum = sum + remainder*remainder*remainder;
  temp = temp/10;
  }
if ( number == sum )
  printf("Entered number is an armstrong number.\n");
  else
  printf("Entered number is not an armstrong number.\n");
  return 0;
  }
```

Output:
```
Enter an integer
371
Entered number is an Armstrong number.
```

Questions

1. What is meant by decision-making structure?
2. Explain following statements with syntax (i) if, (ii) if-else, (iii) switch.
3. What is meant by loop?
4. Explain the for, control structures. Also, explain the role of control variables.
5. Draw a neat syntax diagram of the *if* statement and explain its execution with the help of suitable example.
6. Explain the purpose of switch statement. How does this structure differ from the other structures?
7. Compare switch statement with if-else statement.
8. What will be the output of the following programs.
   (i)
   ```
   main()
   {
       int i;
       for(i=1;i++<=5;printf("%d", i));
   }
   ```
   (ii)
   ```
   main()
   {
       int a = 5;
       do
       {
           printf("%d\n", a);
           a = - 1;
       } while(a>0);
   }
   ```
9. What is the purpose of the while structure? Explain the execution of the while structure.
10. What is the purpose of the do-while structure? How do you distinguish between while and do-while structures?
11. Explain the for, control structures. Also, explain the role of control variables.
12. Write a short note on the nesting of control structures.
13. Write short note on exit().
14. What is the purpose of goto statement?
15. What are the drawbacks of using goto statement in a structured programming language?
16. Describe continue statement with example.
17. Write a program to find average of three number.
18. Explain break statement with example.
19. Write a program to find out factorial of given number.
20. Write a program to display all Armstrong number below 500.
21. Write a program to display first n terms of Fibonacci series.
22. Write a program to print following pattern:
    ```
          *
        *   *
      *   *   *
    *   *   *   *
    ```

■■■

Chapter 4...

Functions and Pointers

Contents ...
4.1 Introduction
    4.1.1 Definition of Function
    4.1.2 Purpose of Function
    4.1.3 What is a Function? / Meaning of Function
    4.1.4 How Function Works?
    4.1.5 Advantages of Functions
    4.1.6 Function Definition
    4.1.7 Function Declaration
    4.1.8 Function Calls
4.2 Types of Functions
4.3 Call by Value and Call by Reference
    4.3.1 Call by Value
    4.3.2 Call by Reference
4.4 Storage Classes
    4.4.1 Auto Storage Class
    4.4.2 Extern Storage Class
    4.4.3 Static Storage Class
    4.4.4 Register Storage Class
4.5 Recursion
4.6 Introduction to Pointers
    4.6.1 Definition of Pointer
    4.6.2 Features of Pointer
    4.6.3 Need of Pointer
    4.6.4 Advantages of Pointer
    4.6.5 Applications of Pointer
    4.6.6 Declaration of Pointer
    4.6.7 Initailization of Pointer
4.7 Indirection Operator and Address of Operator
4.8 Pointer Arithmetic
4.9 Dynamic Memory Allocation
4.10 Functions and Pointers
- Questions

4.1 Introduction

- Functions are the building blocks of C language.
- A number of statements grouped into a single logical unit are called a function.
- A function is a group of statements that together perform a paticular task. Every C program has at least one function which is main(), and all the most trivial programs can define additional functions.
- The use of function makes programming easier since repeated statements can be grouped into functions. Splitting the program into separate function make the program more readable and maintainable.
- C functions can be classified into two types:
  1. Library functions/Built in functions, and
  2. User-defined functions.
- The library functions are the functions which are already defined in C's functions library i.e. header files.
- For example, the functions scanf() and printf() are the library functions defined in file stdio.h same as functions sqrt() is defined in math.h and getch() is defined in conio.h.
- User defined function is the function defined by the programmer who has written the program. The task to perform is decided by the user.
- For example, the main() function is an user-defined function. We decide what is to be written in this function.

4.1.1 Definition of Function

- Function is a set of instructions in a logical sequence, which performs specified task.

OR

- A function is a module or block of program code which deals with a particular task. Making functions is a way of isolating one block of code from other independent blocks of code.

OR

- The function is a self contained block of statements which performs a coherent task of a same kind.

4.1.2 Purpose of Function

- Functions serve two purposes:
  1. They allow a programmer to say: `this piece of code does a specific job which stands by itself and should not be mixed up with anything else',
  2. Second they make a block of code reusable since a function can be reused in many different contexts without repeating parts of the program text.

Need of Functions:

- The functional program facilitates top-down modular programming approach as shown in Fig. 4.1.

- The length of source program can be reduced by using functions at appropriate places.
- It is easy to locate and isolate a faulty function for further investigations.

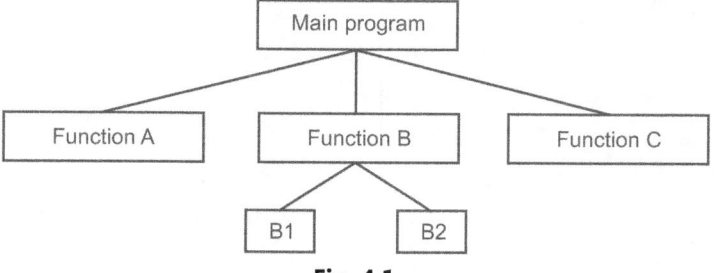

Fig. 4.1

- A function may be used by many other programs. This means that a C programmer can build on what others have already done. That is we can reuse the functions already defined in some program files.

4.1.3 What is a Function? / Meaning of Function

- A function is a self contained program structure.
- A program module or C function has following characteristics:
    1. It has unique name used to identify and invoke by function.
    2. List of parameters called arguments are passed to a function.
    3. Function body has program logic.
    4. Function returns some value in terms of some data type.
- If a program has many (multiple) functions, their definition may appear in any order. Because each function is independent of one another.
- A function will carry the specific action when we access it. The same function can be accessed from many places into the program. When the function action is finished, a program control will returned back to the next statement of a function call.

4.1.4 How Function Works?

- A C language program does not execute the statements in a function until the function is invoked or called.
- When a C program function is called, control passes to the function and returns back to the calling part after the execution of function is over.
- Fig. 4.2 shows function calls and their returns.
- The calling program can send information to the function in the form of argument.
- An argument stores information or data needed by the function to perform its task.
- In C programming functions can send back information to the program in the form of a return value, (See Fig. 4.2).

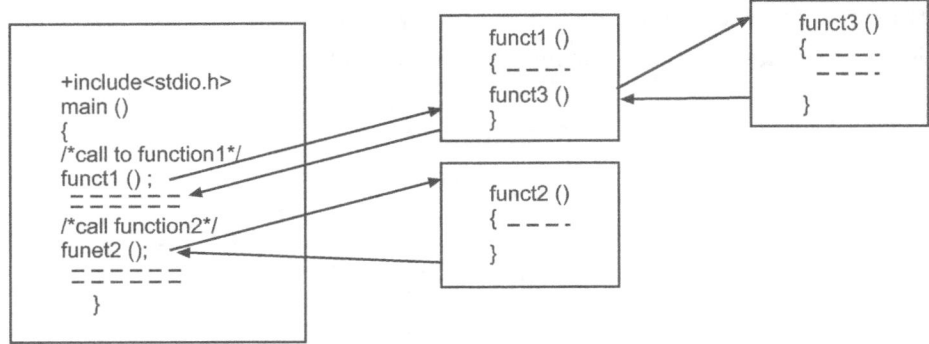

main() calls funct1() and funct2(); funct1() calls funct3()
Fig. 4.2: Working of function

4.1.5 Advantages of Functions

- Various advantages of functions are:
    1. It is easy and simple to use.
    2. Debugging is more suitable for programs.
    3. It reduces the size of a program.
    4. It is easy to understand the actual logic of a program.
    5. Highly suited in case of large programs.
    6. By using functions in a program, it is possible to construct modular and structured programs.
    7. Using functions finding errors becomes easy and simple.

4.1.6 Function Definition

- The function definition is a separate program module that is specially written to implement the requirements of the function.
- So it is also called as function implementation. It includes following:
    o Function Header, and
    o Function Body
- The **general form of function definition** is as given below:

```
function_type function_name(parameters list)}  Function header
    {
    local variables declaration;
    executable statement1;
    executable statement2;
    - - - - - -;
    - - - - - -;
    return statement;
    }
```
                                                Function body

- The first line function_type function_name(parameters list) is known as function header and the statements enclosing the curly braces are known as function body.

1. **Function Header:** It includes three parts:

   (i) **Function type:** It specifies type of the value that the function is expected to return to the program calling the function. It is also called as return type. If function is not returning any values we have to specify it as void.

   (ii) **Function name:** It is any valid C identifier name and therefore must follow the rules for creation of variable names in C.

   (iii) **Parameters list:** It declares variables that will receive the data sent by the calling program. They serve as input data to the function to carry out specific task. Since, they represent the actual input values they are referred as formal parameters or formal arguments.

For example:
```
int find_average(int x, int y int x)
{
--------
}
double square(double x, int n)
{
--------
}
float volume(int a, int b, int c)
{
--------
}
void print_area()
{
--------
}
```

2. **Function Body:** It contains the declarations and statements necessary for performing required task. The body enclosed in braces, contains three parts:

   (i) **Local variables declaration:** It specifies the variables needed by the function locally.

   (ii) **Function statements:** That actually performs task of the function.

   (iii) **The return statement:** It returns the value specified by the function.

- For example:
```
float mul(float x, float y)
{
    float result; /* local variable */
    result = x * y; /* find the result */
    return(result); /* return the result */
}
```

```
void display(void)
{
    printf("Hello World!"); /* only print the value */
}
void sub(int a, int b)
{
    printf("Subtraction: %d", a - b); /* no variables */
    return; /* optional */
}
```

4.1.7 Function Declaration

- Like variables, all functions in C program must be declared, before they are used in calling function. This declaration of function is known as function prototype.
- It is having following syntax:
  ```
  function_type function_name (parameter list);
  ```
  this is very similar to function header except the terminating semicolon.
- For example, the function mul() will be declared as,
  ```
  float mul(float, float);
  ```
- Generally, prototype declarations as not necessary, if the function have been declared before it is used. A prototype declaration may be placed in two places in the program.
  1. Above all the functions, and
  2. Inside function definition.
- We place declaration above all the functions this prototype is known as global prototype. That is, we can use this function in any part on the program.
- When we place the function definition in the local declaration section of another function it is referred as local prototype.

Comparison between Function Definition and Declaration:

Sr. No.	Function Definition	Function Declaration
1.	There is no semicolon at the end of the header.	There is a semicolon at the end of the declaration.
2.	The function body follows the header.	There is no function body.

4.1.8 Function Calls

- A function can be called by simply using function name followed by a list of actual parameters (or arguments) if any, enclosed in parentheses.
- If function is returning any value then we can store the return value in the variable which is of the same data type of that of return value.
- If the function does not return a value, then we declare it to be a function that returns void.

- The **general form of calling the function** is:
    function name(list if arguments);
  when we pass the variables to a function call, the arguments are called actual arguments.
- For example:
    mul(5,3);
- Here, mul is the name of the function, and 5 & 3 are the actual values that we are passing to a function mul.

  Example:
    int mul(int,int);
    void main()
    {
       float m;
       m = mul(5, 3);   /* function call */
       printf("\n%d",m);
    }
- When compiler encounters the function call, it transfers program control to the function mul() by passing values 5 and 3 (actual parameters) to the formal parameters on the function mul().
- The mul() will performs operations on these values and then returns the result. It will be stored in variable m. We are printing the value of variable m on the screen.
- There are a number of different ways in which the function can be called as given below:
    mul(5, 3);
    mul(m, 3);
    mul(5, m);
    mul(m, n);
    mul(m+5, 3);
    mul(m+3, m+9);
    mul(mul(6,8), 4);
- Only we have to remember that the function call must satisfy type and number of arguments passed as parameters to the called function.
- Function call is of two types
  1. **call by value:** When we call function by passing normal values or variables, the function call is called as call by value.
  2. **call by reference:** At the time of function call instead of passing variables or values if we pass the reference of variables then such kind of function call is called as call by reference.

Return Values:
- A function may or may not send back any value to the calling function. If it does, it is done by return statement.
- The return statement also sends the program control back to the calling function.
- It is possible to pass a calling function any number of values but called function can only return one value per call, at most.
- The return statement can take one of the following forms (syntax):

    return;

    OR

    return(value);

    OR

    return(variable);

    OR

    return(expression);

- The first plain return does not return any value; it acts much as closing brace of the function. The remaining three statements can eliminates the brackets also. When the return is executed, the program control immediately transfers back to the calling function. None of the statements written after return are executed afterwards.
- For example:

    return(x);

    printf("Bye…Bye");

- In this case the printf statement will not be executed in any case. Because the return statement will transfer program control immediately back to the calling function.
- Some examples of return are:

    ```
    int div(int x, int y)
    {
       int z;
       z = x / y;
       return z;
    }
    ```

- Here, instead of writing three statements inside the function div(), we can write a single statement as,

    return(x*y);

    OR

    return x*y;

- A function may have more than one return statement when it is associated with any condition such as,

    if(x>y)

    return x;

    else

    return y;

    In this code, in any condition, only one return statement will be executed.

4.2 Types of Functions

- There are two types of functions as:
    1. Built in functions or Pre-defined functions, and
    2. User defined functions.

1. Built in Functions:

- These functions are also called as 'library functions'.
- These functions are provided by system.
- These functions are pre-written, compiled and placed in libraries.
- Various stdio.h library functions are:

Function Name	Prototype	Purpose
1. getchar()	int getchar(void)	gets a character from stdin.
2. putchar()	int putchar(int c)	writes a character to stdout.
3. gets()	char *gets(char *)	gets a string from stdio.
4. puts()	int puts(const char*)	outputs a string to stdout.
5. printf()	int printf(const char* format, [arg, ...]);	writes a character to stdout.
6. scanf()	int scanf(const char* forma, [address, ...]);	scans and formats an input from stdin.
7. sprintf()	int sprintf(char* buffer, char* format, [argument, ...]);	writes formatted output to a string.
8. sscanf()	int sscanf(const char* buffer, const char* format, [address, ...]);	scans and formats input from a string.
9. fflush()	int fflush(file *);	flushes a stream.

Various math.h functions are:

Function Name	Prototype	Purpose
1. abs()	int abs(int x)	Returns the absolute value of x.
2. cos()	double cos(double x)	Returns cosine of x.
3. exp()	double exp(double x)	Calculates ex.
4. floor()	double floor(double x)	Returns the largest integer<=x.
5. log()	double log(double x)	Returns natural log of x.
6. pow()	double pow(double x, double y)	Calculates xy.
7. sin()	double sin(double x)	Calculated sine of x.
8. sqrt()	double sqrt(double x)	Calculates square root of x.

Various conio.h functions are:

Function Name	Prototype	Purpose
1. clrscr()	void clrscr(void)	Clears the text mode window.
2. clreof()	void clreof(void)	Clears to end of line in text window.
3. getch()	int getch(void)	Gets a character from console.
4. getche()	int getche(void)	Same as getch but echoes to screen. No buffering is done.
5. kbhit()	int kbhit(void)	Returns an integer corresponding to a keystroke.
6. putch()	int putch(int ch)	Outputs a character to the text window on screen.

Various stdlib.h functions are:

Function Name	Prototype	Purpose
1. atof()	double atof(const char *s)	Converts a string to float.
2. atoi()	double atoi(const char *s)	Converts a string to int.
3. atoll()	double atoll(const char *s)	Converts a string to long.
4. random()	int random(int num)	Returns an integer between 0 and (num-1).
5. randomize()	void randomized(void)	Initialize the random number generator with a random value.
6. system()	int system(const char* command)	Used to execute an MS-DOS command.

2. User Defined Functions:

- The functions which are created by user for program are known as 'User defined functions'.

Syntax:
```
void main()
{
   // Function prototype
   <return_type><function_name>([<argu_list>]);
   // Function Call
   <function_name>([<arguments>]);
}
// Function definition
<return_type><function_name>([<argu_list>]);
{
   <function_body>;
}
```

Advantages of user defined functions:

- User defined functions helps to decompose the large program into small segments which makes programmar easy to understand, maintain and debug.
- If repeated code occurs in a program. Function can be used to include those codes and execute when needed by calling that function.
- Programmar working on large project can divide the workload by making different functions.

Program 4.1: Program to demonstrate addition of two numbers using function.
```
#include<stdio.h>
#include<conio.h>
void add()
{
   int a, b, c;
   clrscr();
   printf("\n Enter Any 2 Numbers: ");
   scanf("%d %d",&a,&b);
   c = a + b;
   printf("\n Addition is: %d",c);
}
void main()
{
   void add();
   add();
   getch();
}
```
Output:
```
Enter Any 2 Numbers: 23 6
Addition is: 29
```

Categories of the Functions:

- Depending upon whether arguments are present or not and whether value is returned or not functions are categorized as:
    1. Category 1: Functions with no arguments and no return value
    2. Category 2: Functions with arguments and no return value
    3. Category 3: Functions with no arguments and a return value
    4. Category 4: Functions with arguments and a return value

1. Functions with No Arguments and No Return Value:

- In this type of function, the main program will not send any arguments to the calling function and also the function will not return any value to the main program.
- The general form given below is:

    return-type function-name (formal parameter type list);

- Let's see some examples for this category where no arguments will be passed and no value will be returned.

Program 4.2: Write a program to demonstrate the function with no arguments and no return value.

```
#include<stdio.h>
#include<conio.h>
void main( )
{
    clrscr( );
    printf("\n You are welcome to the main program");
    message( );
    printf("\n Welcome back to the main");
}
message( )
{
    printf("\n Welcome to the subprogram");
    return 0;
}
```

Output

```
You are welcome to the main program
Welcome to the subprogram
Welcome back to the main
```

Program 4.3: Write a program to calculate the area of circle.
```
#include<stdio.h>
#include<conio.h>
 void area();   // Prototype Declaration
void main()
{
    clrscr();
    area();
    getch();
}
void area()
{
   float ar; rad;
   printf("nEnter the radius : ");
   scanf("%f",&rad);
   ar = 3.14 * rad * rad ;
   printf("Area of Circle = %f",ar);
}
```
Output
```
Enter the radius: 3
Area of Circle = 28.260000
```

Program 4.4: Write a program to calculate simple interest.
```
#include<stdio.h>
void print_line(void);
void value (void);
   void main()
   {
       print_line();
       value();
       print_line();
   }
void print_line(void)      /* contains no arguments */
  {
       int i ;
       for(i=1; i <= 35; i++)
       printf("%c",'-');
       printf("\n");
   }
```

```
        void value(void)         /* contains no arguments */
        {
            int     year, period;
            float   inrate, sum, principal;
            printf("Principal amount?");
            scanf("%f", &principal);
            printf("Interest rate?   ");
            scanf("%f", &inrate);
            printf("Period?          ");
            scanf("%d", &period);
            sum = principal;
            year = 1;
            while(year <= period)
            {
                sum = sum *(1+inrate);
                year = year +1;
            }
            printf("\n%8.2f %5.2f %5d %12.2f\n",principal,inrate,period,sum);
        }
```

Output:
```
   Principal amount?    5000
   Interest rate?       0.12
   Period?              5
   5000.00  0.12        5        8811.71
```

Program 4.5: Write a program to perform multiplication of two numbers.
```
    #include<stdio.h>
    #include<conio.h>
     void mult();   // Prototype Declaration
    void main()
    {
        clrscr();
        mult();
        getch();
    }
    void mult()
    {
        int res, a,b;
        printf("\n Enter two numbers : ");
        scanf("%d %d",&a,&b);
        res =a*b;
        printf("\n The result is = %d",res);
    }
```
Output:
```
    Enter two numbers : 5 7
    The result is = 35
```

Program 4.6: Write a program to print even numbers up to 30.

```c
#include<stdio.h>
#include<conio.h>
 void even();   // Prototype Declaration
void main()
{
    clrscr();
    even();
    getch();
}
void even()
{
   int i;
   printf("\n Even numbers from 1 to 30 are:");
   for(i=1;i<=30;i++)
   {
        if(i%2==0)
      {
        printf("\t%d",i);
       }
   }
}
```

Output:
2 4 6 8 10 12 14 16 18 20 22 24 26 28 30

2. Functions with Arguments and No Return Value:

- In this type of function, Function accepts argument but it does not return a value back to the calling Program. It is Single (One-way) Type Communication.
- The **general form** for a function declaration:

    return-type function-name (formal parameter type list);

- A void functions with value parameters are declared by enclosing the list of types for the parameter list in the parentheses.
- In this type of category of functions we pass arguments as an actual arguments and the called function receive these values in its definition as formal parameters. But nothing will be returned by the called function to the calling function.
- The number of actual parameter should be equal to the formal parameters and also the data type of both the parameter should be same. Let's see some examples for this category where arguments will be passed and no value will be returned.

Program 4.7: Write a program to demonstrate the functions with arguments and no return value.

```
#include<stdio.h>
#include<conio.h>
void main()
{
int a,b;
printf("\n Enter a value for a :");
scanf("%d",&a);
printf("\n Enter a value for b :");
scanf("%d",&b);
funct(a,b);
getch();
}
funct(int a1, int b1)
{
int c;
c=a1+b1;
printf("\n Result = %d",c);
return 0;
}
```

Output:
```
Enter a value for a : 12
Enter a value for b : 10
Result = 22
```

Program 4.8: Write a program to find the average of the three numbers.

```
#include<stdio.h>
#include<conio.h>
void main()
{
    int a,b,c;
printf("\n Enter a value for a :");
scanf("%d",&a);
printf("\n Enter a value for b :");
scanf("%d",&b);
printf("\n Enter a value for c :");
scanf("%d",&c);
average(a,b,c);
getch();
}
```

```
average(int a1, int b1, int c1)
{
int avg;
avg=(a1+b1+c1)/3;
printf("\n Average is  = %d",avg);
return 0;
}
```
Output:
```
Enter a value for a : 12
Enter a value for b : 10
Enter a value for c : 8
Average is = 10
```

Program 4.9: Write a program to print all prime numbers up to the number entered by user.
```
#include<stdio.h>
#include<conio.h>
void main()
{
   int n;
   printf("\n Enter the limit :");
   scanf("%d",&n);
   prime(n);
   getch()
}
void prime(int limit)
{
int i,j,flag;
for(i=2;i<=limit;i++)
{
   flag=0;
   for(j=2;j<=i/2;j++)
   {
      if(i%j==0)
      {
         flag=1;
         break;
      }
      if(flag==0)
      printf("\t%d",i);
   }
}
}
```
Output:
```
Enter the limit: 10
 2   3   5   7
```

Program 4.10: Write a program to print square root of a number entered by user.

```c
#include<stdio.h>
#include<conio.h>
#include<math.h>
void main()
{
    int a;
    printf("\n Enter the number :");
    scanf("%d",&a);
    root(a);
    getch();
}
void root(int num)
{
    int res;
    res = sqrt(num);
    printf("The square root of a number is :%d",res);
}
```

Output:

```
Enter the number : 27
The square root of a number is : 9
```

Program 4.11: Write a program to accept character from user and check whether it is vowel or not.

```c
#include<stdio.h>
#include<conio.h>
void vowel(char ch);
void main()
{
    char ch;
    printf("\n Enter the character :");
    scanf("%c",&val);
    vowel(ch);
    getch();
}
```

```
void vowel(char ch)
{
    if (ch == 'a' || ch == 'A' || ch == 'e' || ch == 'E' || ch == 'i'
    || ch == 'I' || ch =='o' || ch=='O' || ch == 'u' || ch == 'U')
    printf("%c is a vowel.\n", ch);
    else
    printf("%c is not a vowel.\n", ch);
}
```

Output:
```
Enter the character : o
o is a vowel
```

3. **Functions with no Arguments and a Return Value:**
- In this type of function, the calling program will not send any arguments to the called function but the called function will return the value to the calling function.
- The **general form** is given below:
    return-type function-name (formal parameter type list);
- Let's see some examples for this category where no arguments will be passed and value will be returned.

Program 4.12: Write a program to demonstrate the Functions with no arguments but returns a value.

```
#include<stdio.h>
#include<conio.h>
int send()
{
    int no;
    printf("\n Enter a number : ");
    scanf("%d",&no);
    return(no);
}
 void main()
{
    int z;
    clrscr();
    z = send();
    printf("\nYou entered : %d.", z);
    getch();
}
```

Output:
```
Enter a number : 25
You entered : 25
```

Program 4.13: Write a program to add digits of a number entered by user.

```c
#include<stdio.h>
#include<conio.h>
int sum()
{
    int no, res=0, remainder;
    printf("\n Enter a number : ");
    scanf("%d",&no);
    while(no != 0)
    {
       remainder = no % 10;
       res = res + remainder;
       no = no / 10;
    }
    return(res);
}
 void main()
{
    int z;
    clrscr();
    z = sum();
    printf("\n The sum of  the digits is : %d.", z);
    getch();
}
```

Output:
```
Enter a number : 1234
The sum of the digits is : 10
```

4. **Functions with arguments and a Return Value:**
- This type of function can send arguments (data) from the calling function to the called function and wait for the result to be returned back from the called function back to the calling function.
- And this type of function is mostly used in programming world because it can do two way communications; it can accept data as arguments as well as can send back data as return value.
- Let's see some examples for this category where arguments will be passed and value will be returned.

Program 4.14: Program to demonstrate the Functions with arguments and returns a value.

```c
#include<stdio.h>
#include<conio.h>
 int add(int x, int y)
{
    int result;
    result = x+y;
    return(result);
}
void main()
{
    int z;
    clrscr();
     z = add(952,321);
    printf("Result %d.\n\n",add(30,55));
    printf("Result %d.\n\n",z);
     getch();
}
```

Output:
```
Result 85
Result 1273
```

Program 4.15: Program to find hcf (highest common factor) and lcm (least common multiple).

```c
#include <stdio.h>
#include <conio.h>
long gcd(long, long);
void main()
{
  long x, y, hcf, lcm;
  clrscr();
  printf("Enter two integers\n");
  scanf("%ld%ld", &x, &y);
  hcf = gcd(x, y);
  lcm = (x*y)/hcf;
  printf("Greatest common divisor of %ld and %ld = %ld\n", x, y, hcf);
  printf("Least common multiple of %ld and %ld = %ld\n", x, y, lcm);
  getch();
}
```

```c
long gcd(long x, long y)
 {
  if (x == 0)
  {
    return y;
  }
  while (y != 0)
  {
    if (x > y)
    {
      x = x - y;
    }
    else
    {
      y = y - x;
    }
  }
    return x;
 }
```

Output:
```
Enter two integers
9 15
Greatest common divisor of 9 and 15 = 3
Least common multiple of 9 and 15 = 45
```

Program 4.16: Program to find factorial of a number.
```c
#include <stdio.h>
#include<conio.h>
long factorial(int);
void main()
{
  int number;
  long fact
  clrscr();
  printf("\n Enter a number to calculate it's factorial : ");
  scanf("%d", &number);
  printf("\n The factorial of a number is :%d", factorial(number));
  getch();
}
```

```
  long factorial(int n)
{
  int j;
  long result = 1;
  for (j = 1; j <= n; j++)
  result = result * j;
  return result;
}
```
Output:
```
Enter a number to calculate it's factorial : 5
The factorial of a number is : 120
```

4.3 Call by Value and Call by Reference
4.3.1 Call by Value
- The transfer of values between the actual and formal parameter takes place by call by value.
- In this case the values get passed through actual parameter to formal parameter when a function gets called. In this case only one value can be returned.
- When a function is called by value of variables then that function is known as 'function call by values.'
- Function in C passes all arguments by value. When a single value is passed to a function via an actual argument, the value of the actual argument is copied into the function.
- Therefore, the value of the corresponding formal argument can be altered within the function, but the value of the actual argument within the calling routine will not change. This procedure for passing the value of an argument to a function is known as passing by value.

Syntax:
```
    // Declaration
    void <function_name>(<data_type><var_nm>);
    // Calls
    <function_name>(<var_nm>);
    // Definition
    void <function_name>(<data_type><var_nm>);
    {
       <function_body>;
       - - - - - - - -;
    }
```

Program 4.17: Program for call by value.

```c
#include<stdio.h>
#include<conio.h>
int add(int p,int q);
int main()
{
    int a,b,c;
    clrscr();
    printf("Enter two numbers \n");
    scanf("%d %d", &a, &b);
    c = add(a,b);
    printf("\nSum of %d and %d is %d", a, b, c);
    getch();
    return 0;
}
int add(int p, int q)
{
    int result;
    result=p+q;
    return(result);
}
```

Output:
```
Enter two numbers
10
20
Sum of 10 20 is 30
```

4.3.2 Call by Reference

- In call by reference method, the address of an argument is copied into the parameter.
- Call by reference can be achieved by passing a pointer to an argument. As we pass address of the argument, the code within the function can change the value of the arguments outside the function.
- Pass by Reference mechanism is used when you want a function to do the changes in passed parameters and reflect those changes back to the calling function. In this case only addresses of the variables are passed to a function so that function can work directly over the addresses.

Program 4.18: Program for call by reference.
```
#include<stdio.h>
#include<conio.h>
void add(int *p, int *q, int *r);
void main()
{
    int a,b,c;
    clrscr();
    printf("Enter two numbers \n");
    scanf("%d %d", &a, &b);
    add(&a, &b, &c);
    printf("\nSum of %d and %d is %d", a, b, c);
    getch();
}
void add(int *p, int *q, int *r)
{
    *r = *p + *q;
}
```
Output:
```
Enter two numbers
10
20
Sum of 10 20 is 30
```

Difference between call by value and call by reference:

Call by value	Call by reference
1. This is the usual method to call a function in which only the value of the variable is passed as an argument	1. In this method, the address of the variable is passed as an argument
2. Any alternation in the value of the argument passed is local to the function and is not accepted in the calling program	2. Any alternation in the value of the argument passed is accepted in the calling program(since alternation is made indirectly in the memory location using the pointer)
3. Memory location occupied by formal and actual arguments is different	3. Memory location occupied by formal and actual arguments is same and there is a saving of memory location
4. Since a new location is created, this method is slow	4. Since the existing memory location is used through its address, this method is fast
5. There is no possibility of wrong data manipulation since the arguments are directly used in an application	5. There is a possibility of wrong data manipulation since the addresses are used in an expression. A good skill of programming is required here

4.4 Storage Classes

- 'Storage' refers to the scope of a variable and memory allocated by compiler to store that variable.
- Scope of a variable is the boundary within which a variable can be used.
- Storage class defines the scope and lifetime of a variable.
- We can define scope of a variable as, the region of the program in which the variable is valid or visible.
- Storage class refers to the manner in which memory is allocated by the compile to variables.
- A storage class defines the scope (visibility) and life time of variables and/or functions within a C Program.
- It determines the scope and lifetime of a variable. There are two types of locations in a computer where such a value stored one is Memory and another is CPU registers.
- There are four types of storage classes:
    1. Automatic,
    2. Register,
    3. Static, and
    4. External.
- The storage class of a variable answers the following questions:
    1. Where the variable would be stored?
    2. What will be the default initial value?
    3. What is the scope of the variable?
    4. How long would the variable exist?

4.4.1 Auto Storage Class

- These classes are created when the function is called and destroyed automatically when the function is exited.
- Auto storage class is the default for local variables.
  Syntax: auto [data_type] [variable_name];
  Example:
  ```
  int num(int n)
  {
      int count;
      auto int Employee;
  }
  ```
- Above example defines two variables with the same storage class auto class can only be used within functions, i.e. local variables.

- The auto variables are created when the function is called and declared automatically when the function is exited.
- The life of value of variable depends on the storage class a variable may assume. The variable in C can have any one of the four storage classes.
- **Automatic Variables:** They are declared inside a function in which they are to bed utilized. They are created when the function is called and destroyed automatically when the function is exited, hence the name automatic. Automatic variables are also referred to as local or internal variables. When a variable is declared inside a function without storage class, by default, it is an automatic variable. The keyword 'auto' is used to declare automatic variables.
- One important feature of automatic variable is that their value cannot be changed accidentally.

Features of Auto Storage Classes:

1. Scope : Local to the block in which it is defined.
2. Default initial value : Garbage value
3. Life : Till the control remains within the block where it is defined
4. Storage : Memory

Program 4.19: Program to demonstrate automatic storage class.

```c
#include<stdio.h>
#include<conio.h>
void main()
{
   auto int i=10;
   clrscr();
   {
      auto int i=20;
      printf("\n\t %d",i);
   }
   printf("\n\n\t %d",i);
   getch();
}
```

Output:

```
20
10
```

4.4.2 Extern Storage Class

- Extern is used to give a reference of a global variable that is visible to ALL the program files.
- When you use 'extern' the variable cannot be initalized as all it does is point the variable name at a storage location that has been previously defined.
- Extern storage class defines a global variable that is accessible by any function in the program. This class are declared outside all functions.
  Syntax: `extern [data_type] [variable_name];`
  Example: `extern int a;`
- The variable access time is very fast as compared to other storage classes. But few registers are available for user programs.
- The variables of this class can be referred to as 'global or external variables.' They are declared outside the functions and can be invoked at anywhere in a program.
- External variables: Variables that are both alive and active throughout the entire program are known as external variables. They are also known as Global variables. These variables can be accessed by any function in the program. They are declared outside the function. The keyword 'extern' can be used to declare a variable inside the function main.
- In some cases, the same global variable defined in file X is used again in file Y. Then how does the compiler know that the variable used in file Y is actually the same variable declared in file X.
- The answer is, use the extern specifier to the global variable defined elsewhere. In this condition, we declare a global variable in file X, and then declare the variable again using the extern specifier in file Y.
- For example, suppose we have two global int variables, a and b, that are defined in one file, and then in another file, you may have the following declarations.

```
int a = 0;        /* a is a global variable */
extern int b;     /* an allusion to a global variable y */
int main( )
{
   extern int c;  /* an allusion to a global variable z */
   int I;         /* I is a local variable */
   .
   .
   return 0;
}
```

Features of Extern – storage class are listed below:
1. Scope : Global
2. Storage : Memory
3. Life : Active throughout the entire program
4. Default initial value : Zero

Program 4.20: Program to demonstrate external storage class.
```c
#include<stdio.h>
#include<conio.h>
extern int i=10;
void main()
{
   int i=20;
   void show(void);
   clrscr();
   printf("\n\t %d",i);
   show();
   getch();
}
void show(void)
{
   printf("\n\n\t %d",i);
}
```
Output:
```
20
10
```

4.4.3 Static Storage Class

- Static storage class is the default for global variables. The two variables i.e. count and road in the following example have a static storage class.
- Static storage class can be used only if we want the value of a variable to persist between different function calls.
   Syntax: static [data_type] [variable_name];
   For example,
   ```c
   data int count;
   int road;
   main( )
      {
         printf("%d\n", count);
         printf("%d\n", road);
      }
   ```
- **Static variables:** The value of static variables persists until the end of the program. A variable can be declared static using the keyword 'static' like static int x. A static variable may be either an internal type or an external type, depending on the place of declaration. Internal static variable can be used to retain values between function calls. Static variable is initialized only once, when program is compiled.

- Static storage class can also be defined to local variables and they retain their values between calls to the function.

   For example:
   ```
   void Func(void)
   {
      static count=1;
   }
   ```

Features of static storage class for listed below:

1. Scope   : Local to the block in which it is defined
2. Default initial value : Zero
3. Storage   : Memory
4. Life   : Persists between different function calls.

Program 4.21: Program to demonstrate static storage class.
```
#include<stdio.h>
#include<conio.h>
void main()
{
   int i;
   void incre(void);
   clrscr();
   for (i=0; i<3; i++)
   incre();
   getch();
}
void incre(void)
{
   int avar=1;
   static int svar=1;
   avar++;
   svar++;
   printf("\n\n Automatic variable value: %d",avar);
   printf("\t Static variable value: %d",svar);
}
```
Output:
```
Automatic variable value: 2      Static variable value: 2
Automatic variable value: 2      Static variable value: 3
Automatic variable value: 2      Static variable value: 4
```

4.4.4 Register Storage Class

- Register storage class is used to define local variables that should be stored in a CPU register instead of memory i.e. the variable has a maximum equal to the register size and can't have the unary '&' operates applied to it.
  Syntax: `register [data_type] [variable_name];`
- Register is used to define local variables that should be stored in a register instead of RAM.
- **Register variables:** We can tell the compiler that a variable should be kept in one of the machine's register, instead of keeping in memory. Since a register access is much faster than a memory access, keeping the frequently accessed variables in the register will lead to faster execution of programs. These variables can be declared as,
  `register int count;`
- Since, only a few variables can be placed in the register, it is important to carefully select the variables for this purpose otherwise C will automatically convert register variables into non-register variables, once limit is reached.
  For example:
  ```
  {
      register int items;
  }
  ```

Features of Register-storage class are given below:

1. Scope   : Local to the block in which it is defined
2. Storage   : CPU registers
3. Life   : Till the control remains within the block where it is defined
4. Default initial value : Garbage value.

Program 4.22: Program to demonstrate register storage class.

```c
#include <stdio.h>
#include <conio.h>
void main()
{
    register int i=10;
    clrscr();
    {
        register int i=20;
        printf("\n\t %d",i);
    }
    printf("\n\n\t %d",i);
    getch();
}
```

Output:
```
20
10
```

Comparison of Storage Classes:

Features	Automatic Storage Class	Register Storage Class	Static Storage Class	External Storage Class
Keyword	auto	register	static	extern
Initial Value	Garbage	Garbage	Zero	Zero
Storage	Memory	CPU register	Memory	Memory
Scope	scope limited, local to block	scope limited, local to block	scope limited, local to block	Global
Life	limited life of block, where defined	limited life of block, where defined	value of variable persist between different function calls	Global, till the program execution
Memory location	Stack	Register memory	Segment	Segment

Example	`void main()`
	`{`
	`auto int i;`
	`printf("%d",i);`
	`}`
	Output:
	124
		`void main()`
		`{`
		`register int i;`
		`for(i=1; i<=5 ; i++);`
		`printf("%d ",i);`
		`}`
		Output:
		1 2 3 4 5
			`void add();`
			`void main()`
			`{`
			`    add();`
			`    add();`
			`}`
			`void add()`
			`{`
			`static int i=1;`
			`printf("\n%d",i);`
			`i=i+1;`
			`}`
			Output:
			1
			2
				`void main()`
				`{`
				`extern int i;`
				`printf("%d",i);`
				`int i=5`
				`}`
				Output:
				0

4.5 Recursion

- A function that calls itself is known as recursive function and the process of calling function itself is known as recursion in C programming.
- Recursive functions are those functions, which call itself within that function.
- In short Recursion refers to the process in which a function calls itself.
- A recursive function must have the following type of statements.
    1. A statement to test and determine whether the function is calling itself again.
    2. A statement that calls the function itself and must be argument.
    3. A conditional statement (if-else)
    4. A return statement.

Features of recursion:
1. There should be at least one if statement used to terminate recursion.
2. It does not contain any looping statements.

- Recursion is the process of repeating items in a self-similar way. Same applies in programming languages as well where if a programming allows you to call a function inside the same function that is called recursive call of the function as follows.

For example:
```
void recursion()
{
 recursion(); /* function calls itself */
}
int main()
{
 recursion();
}
```

Program 4.23: Program to generates fibonacci series for a given number using a recursive function:
```
#include <stdio.h>
int fibonacci(int i)
{
 if(i == 0)
 {
 return 0;
 }
 if(i == 1)
 {
 return 1;
 }
 return fibonacci(i-1) + fibonacci(i-2);
}
int main()
{
 int i;
 for (i = 0; i < 10; i++)
 {
 printf("%d\t%n", fibonacci(i));
 }
 return 0;
}
```
Output:
```
0  1  1  2  3  5  8  13  21  34
```

Program 4.24: To calculate factorial using recursion.
```
#include<stdio.h>
int factorial(int n);
int main()
{
 int n;
 printf("Enter an positive integer: ");
 scanf("%d",&n);
 printf("Factorial of %d = %ld", n, factorial(n));
 return 0;
}
int factorial(int n)
{
 if(n!=1)
 return n*factorial(n-1);
}
```
Output:
```
Enter an positive integer: 6
Factorial of 6 = 720
```

Program 4.25: Program to display prime numbers between intervals by using function.
```
#include<stdio.h>
int check_prime(int num);
int main()
{
 int n1,n2,i,flag;
 printf("Enter two numbers(intervals): ");
 scanf("%d %d",&n1, &n2);
 printf("Prime numbers between %d and %d are: ", n1, n2);
 for(i=n1+1;i<n2;++i)
 {
 flag=check_prime(i);
 if(flag==0)
 printf("%d ",i);
 }
 return 0;
}
```

```c
int check_prime(int num) /* User-defined function to check prime number*/
{
 int j,flag=0;
 for(j=2;j<=num/2;++j){
 if(num%j==0){
 flag=1;
 break;
 }
 }
 return flag;
}
```

Output:
```
Enter two numbers(intervals): 10
30
Prime numbers between 10 and 30 are: 11 13 17 19 23 29
```

Program 4.26: Program to check prime and armstrong number by using function.

```c
#include <stdio.h>
int prime(int n);
int armstrong(int n);
int main()
{
 char c;
 int n,temp=0;
 printf("Eneter a positive integer: ");
 scanf("%d",&n);
 printf("Enter P to check prime and A to check Armstrong number: ");
 c=getche();
 if (c=='p' || c=='P')
 {
 temp=prime(n);
 if(temp==1)
 printf("\n%d is a prime number.", n);
 else
 printf("\n%d is not a prime number.", n);
 }
```

```c
    if (c=='a' || c=='A')
    {
    temp=armstrong(n);
    if(temp==1)
    printf("\n%d is an Armstrong number.", n);
    else
    printf("\n%d is not an Armstrong number.",n);
    }
    return 0;
}
int prime(int n)
{
 int i, flag=1;
 for(i=2; i<=n/2; ++i)
 {
 if(n%i==0)
 {
 flag=0;
 break;
 }
 }
 return flag;
}
int armstrong(int n)
{
 int num=0, temp, flag=0;
 temp=n;
 while(n!=0)
 {
 num+=(n%10)*(n%10)*(n%10);
 n/=10;
 }
 if (num==temp)
 flag=1;
 return flag;
}
```

Output
```
Enter a positive integer: 371
Enter P to check prime and A to check Armstrong number: p
371 is not a prime number.
```

Advantages:
It is easy to use.
It represents compact programming structures.
Disadvantage:
1. It is slower than that of looping statements because each time function is called,

Program 4.27: Write a program to find sum of digits using recursion.

```
#include<stdio.h>
#include<conio.h>
void main()
{
  int num,x;
  clrscr();
  printf("\n.Enter a number: ");
  scanf("%d",&num);
  x=findsum(num);
  printf("\n Sum of the digits of %d is: %d",num,x);
  getch();
}
int r,s;
int findsum(int n)
{
if(n)
{
   r=n%10;
   s=s+r;
   findsum(n/10);
}
else
return s;
}
```

Output:
```
Enter a number: 2342
Sum of the digits of 2342 is: 11
```

Program 4.28: Write a program to Find power of a number using recursion.

```
#include<stdio.h>
#include<conio.h>
void main()
{
  int pow,num;
  long int res;
  long int power(int,int);
  clrscr();
  printf("\n Enter a number: ");
  scanf("%d",&num);
  printf("\n Enter power: ");
  scanf("%d",&pow);
  res=power(num,pow);
  printf("\n%d to the power %d is: %ld",num,pow,res);
  getch();
}
  int i=1;
  long int sum=1;
  long int power(int num,int pow)
{
if(i<=pow)
{
   sum=sum*num;
   power(num,pow-1);
}
else
return sum;
}
```

Output:
```
Enter a number: 5
Enter power: 3
5 to the power 3 is 125
```

4.6 Introduction to Pointers

- A pointer is a variable that holds a memory address. This memory address is the location of another object in memory.
- For example, if one variable contain the address of another variable, the first variable is said to point the second variable.
- Pointers are used in C program to access the memory and manipulate the address. Fig. 4.3 shows the above situation.

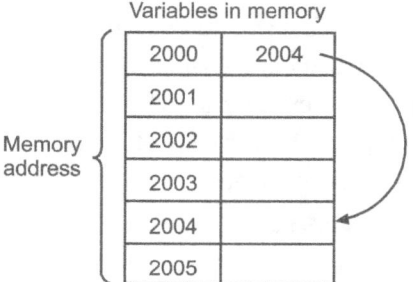

Fig. 4.3

- A pointer is a variable that represents the address (location) of a data item in the computer's memory.
- Every data item is stored in memory, occupies a space somewhere in memory.
- Pointer is a variable which holds the memory address of another variable.
- Pointers are represented by '*'. It is a derive data type in C.
- Pointer returns the value of stored address.

   Syntax: `<data_type> * pointer_name;`

4.6.1 Definition of Pointer

- A pointer is a variable that stores the memory address of another variable.

OR

- A pointer is a variable that represents the location (rather than the value) of a data item such as a variable or an array element.

OR

- Pointers are the variables that contain the address of another variable within the memory.

4.6.2 Features of Pointer

- Features of pointer are listed below:
    1. Pointer variable should have prefix '*'.
    2. Combination of data types is not allowed.
    3. Pointers are more effective and useful in handling arrays.

4. It can also be used to return multiple values from a function using function arguments.
5. It supports dynamic memory management.
6. It reduces complexity and length of a program.
7. It helps to improve execution speed that results in reducing program execution time.

4.6.3 Need of Pointers

- Following points describes need of pointers:
    1. Pointer is used for creating data structures such as linked lists, trees, graphs etc.
    2. Pointer enhances the capability of the language to manipulate data.
    3. Pointers allows working with dynamically allocated memory.
    4. Pointers reduce the length and complexity of the program.
    5. Pointers increases the execution speed.

4.6.4 Advantages of Pointers

- Pointer consists of the following advantages:
    1. Pointers provide an alternate way to access individual array element.
    2. Pointers provide a convenient way to represent multi-dimensional arrays, allowing a single multidimensional array to be replaced by a lower-dimensional array of pointers.
    3. Pointers are more efficient in handling complex data structures and data tables.
    4. Pointers reduce the length of a program.
    5. Pointers increase the program execution speed.

4.6.5 Applications of Pointers

- Applications of pointers are listed below:
    1. Pointers can be used to simulate passing parameters by reference i.e. the arguments can be modified.
    2. They provide an alternate method to access array elements.
    3. They are used for passing arrays and strings to functions.
    4. They are more efficient in handling complex data structures like linked lists, trees, graphs, etc.
    5. One of the most important use of pointer is a dynamic memory allocation where memory is allocated and released for a variable during run-time.

4.6.6 Declaration of Pointer

- Pointer variables must be declared before they may be used in a C program.
- When a pointer variable is declared, the variable name must be proceeded by an asterisk (*) sign.
- This identifies the fact that the variable is a pointer. The data type that appears in the declaration refers to the object of the pointer.

- **Syntax** for pointer are given below:

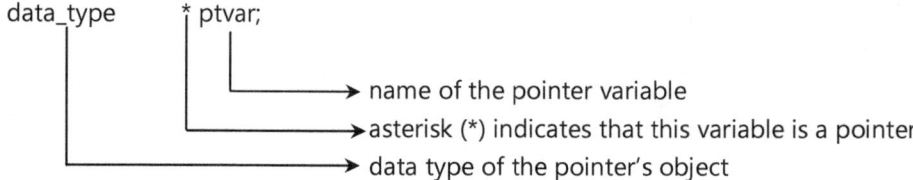

- Above syntax tells the compiler that:
  1. ptvar is a pointer.
  2. ptvar needs memory location.
  3. ptvar points to a variable of type data_type.

OR

    data_type * pointer_name;

where, data types is C datatype and pointer_name is name of pointer which is a valid C identifiers.

Example:

    int *p;   // declares that 'p' is a pointer that points to an integer data type.
    float *xyz;   // declares that 'xyz' is a pointer that points to a floating point
                    variable.
    char *pragati; // declares that 'status' is a pointer that points to a char variable.

4.6.7 Initialisation of Pointer

- The process of assigning the address of a variable to a pointer variable is known as initialization.
- After declaration, we have to initialize the pointer variable. Use of the 'address of (&)' operator as a prefix to the variable name assigns its address to the pointer.
- **General form of pointer initialization** is given below:

    pointer=&variable;

Example:

    iptr = &zvar;   // assigns the address of variable 'zvar' to pointer 'zptr'

- We can also assign a pointer value to another variable of the same type.

Example:

    int z = 5, x, *zptr;
    aptr = &z;   // assigns the address of variable 'z' to the pointer 'zptr'
    x = *zptr;   // assigns the value at the address pointed by 'zptr' to variable x i.e. x = 5
    zptr = 0   // assigns value 0 to 'z' since z = *zptr

The two statements,

    zptr = &z;
    x = *zptr;

are equivalent to single statement,

    x = *(&z);

or   x = z;

- That is, the & operator is the inverse of *operator.

Program 4.29: Program which demonstrates the declaration of pointer.
```c
#include<stdio.h>
main( )
{
   int l = 2;
   int * m;
   m = &l;
   printf("\n Address of l = %u", m);
   printf("\n Value of l = %d", * m);
}
```
Output:
```
Address of l = 65524
Value of l = 2
```

4.7 Indirection Operator and Address of Operator

1. Indirection Operator (*):
- The value of variable using pointer can be accessed using unary operator * (asterisk), known as the indirection operator or dereferencing operator.
- De-referencing is the operation performed to access data contained in the memory location pointed by the pointer.

    For example:
    ```
    int d1, d2, *p;
    d1=30;
    p=&d1;
    d2=*p;
    ```

- In above statements d1, d2 are integer variables and p is a integer pointer variable. The value 30 is stored in variable d1. Then the address of variable d1 is stored into p. The *p returns the value of variable d1, which is stored into variable d2. That means the above statements copies the value of variable d1 into variable d2.
- The statements,
    ```
    p=&d1;
    d2=*p;
    ```
    are equivalent to the following single statement,
    ```
    d2=* &d1;
    ```
    which is equivalent to,
    ```
    d2 = d1;
    ```
- The unary operator '&' gives the address of a variable.
- The unary operator '*' gives the value of address.

Program 4.30: Program to illustrate the use if dereferencing or indirection operator '*'.

```
#include<stdio.h>
void main()
{
   int d1=30, *p;
   p=&d1;
   printf("\nThe value of d1=%d",d1);
   printf("\nThe address of d1=%u",p);
   printf("\nThe value of d1=%d",*p);
   printf("\nThe value of d1=%d", * &d1);
   return 0;
}
```

Output:
```
The value of d1=30
The address of d1=65524
The value of d1=30
The value of d1=30
```

2. Address of Operator (&):

- The address operator (&) must act upon operands that associated with unique address, such as ordinary variable or single array element. Thus the address operators cannot act upon arithmetic expressions.

Program 4.31: Program for & operator.

```
#include <stdio.h>
int main()
{
 int *ptr, q;
 q = 50;
 /* address of q is assigned to ptr */
 ptr = &q;
 /* display q's value using ptr variable */
 printf("%d", *ptr);
 return 0;
}
```

Output:
```
50
```

4.8 Pointer Arithmetic

- Number of operations can be performed on pointers since they are variables. Here, we see the following operations perform on a pointers.
    1. Increment-decrement.
    2. Adding a number from a pointer.
    3. Subtracting a number from a pointer.
    4. Subtraction of one pointer from another.
    5. Comparison of two pointer variables.
- But some operations seem absurd and would give unpredictable results if performed.

1. Increment-Decrement:

- Suppose pt is a pointer pointing to integer type of data. i.e.

    int * pt;
- If we give pt++ then it increments pt to point to next location of same type. What do we mean by same type? If pt is a pointer to integer, integers occupy 2 bytes. So if pt = 4001, pt++ gives pt = 4003. If it points char data then it will move 1 bytes ahead.

  pt-- decrements pt to point to previous element of the same type.
- Suppose char type data need 1 byte and int type data need 2 bytes. So when a char pointer is incremented its value increase by 1 and when a int pointer is incremented its value increases by 2 or the increment will take according to the base type it points. One can even add or subtract integers from pointer values.

    For example:

    int * a;

    a = a + a;

    is also valid.
- Also subtraction of one pointer from another only makes sense when both pointers point to a common object, such as an array. The subtraction then yield number of elements of the base type separating the two pointers values.
- Apart from these operation no other arithmetic operation is valid on pointers. We cannot multiply or divide pointers. We cannot add two pointers.

    For example:

    char * ch = 3000;

    int * i = 3001;

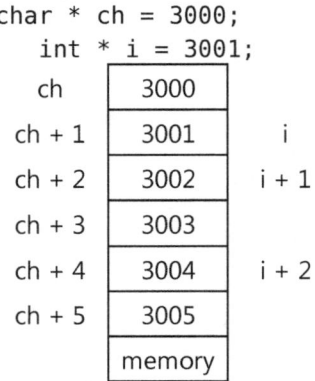

2. **Adding a number to a pointer:**

   A number can be added to a pointer.

   For example:
   ```
   int i = 3, * j;
      j = & i;
      j = j + 1;
      j = j + 9;
   ```
   In line no. 4, j points to 9 integer locations after current location.

3. **Subtracting a number from a pointer:**

   A number can be subtracted from a pointer.

   For example:
   ```
   int i = 3, * j;
      j = & i;
      j = j - 2;
      j = j - 6;
   ```
   In line no. 4, j points to 6 integer locations before current location.

4. **Subtraction of one pointer from another:**

   One pointer variable can be subtracted from another, provided both point to elements of same array. The result is the number of elements between corresponding array elements.

Program 4.32: Program to subtract one pointer from another pointer.
```
#include<stdio.h>
main( )
{
   int arr [ ] = {10, 20, 30, 45, 67, 56, 74};
   int * i, * j;
   i = & arr [1];
   j = & arr [5];
   printf("%d %d", j - i, * j - * i);
   return 0;
}
```
Output:

504/36

Here, (j – 1) gives the difference between addresses.

(*j – *i) gives the difference between values contained in addresses at j & i.

5. **Comparison of two pointer variables:**

   Comparison of two pointer variables is possible provided both point to one array (i.e. both pointers point to objects of same data type).

   Pointers can also be compared with zero (NULL).

Program 4.33: Program to compare two pointers variables.
```
#include<stdio.h>
main( )
{
    int arr [ ] = {10, 20, 36, 72, 35, 36};
    int *j, *k;
    j = &arr [4];
    k = (arr + 4);
    if(j = ^ k)
        printf("\n The two pointers point to same location");
    else
        printf("\n The two pointers do not point to same location");
    return 0;
}
```
Output:
```
The two pointers point to same location.
```

> **Note:** The operations of adding two pointers, multiplication of a pointer with a constant, division of a pointer with a constant should not be performed.

6. **Pointer Expressions:**
- Pointer variables can be used in expressions like other variables.

    For example:
    (i)   a = (* pt1) * (* pt2);
    (ii) s = s + *p1;
    (iii) * p2 = * p2 + 15;
    (iv) c + = * p3;
    Here, we see that ' = ' assignment operator can be used on pointers.

Program 4.34: Write a program for pointer expression.
```
/* Program of pointer expression */
#include<stdio.h>
main( )
{
    int a = 12; * p;
    p = &a;
    *p = *p + 3;
    printf("%u %d", p, *p);
    getch ();
    return 0;
}       /* end of main */
```
Output:
```
6552415
```

Program 4.35: Program to demonstrate the arithmetical operation pointers.

```c
#include<stdio.h>
void main( )
{
   char c='1',*cp;
   floatf=10.2,*fp;
   int i=987,*ip;
   long l=345,*lp;
   cp=&c,fp=&f,ip=&lp,lp=&1;
   printf("\n Char float int long");
   printf("\n%8x%8x%8x%8x%",cp,fp,ip,lp");
   for(i=0;i<3;i++)
   {
      cp++;fp++;ip++lp++;
      printf("\n%8x%8x%8x%8x%8x%",cp,fp,ip,lp");
   }
   for(i=0;i<3;i++)
   {  cp--;fp--;ip--;lp--;
      printf("\n8x%8x%8x%8x%",cp,fp,ip,lp");
   }
}
```

4.9 Dynamic Memory Allocation

- Dynamic memory allocation allows a program to obtain more memory space, while running or to release space when no space is required.
- Although, C language inherently does not has any technique to allocated memory dynamically, there are 4 library functions under "stdlib.h" for dynamic memory allocation.

1. malloc()	Allocates requested size of bytes and returns a pointer first byte of allocated space.
2. calloc()	Allocates space for an array elements, initializes to zero and then returns a pointer to memory.
3. free()	dellocate the previously allocated space.
4. realloc()	Change the size of previously allocated space.

1. **malloc():** The name malloc stands for "memory allocation". The function malloc() reserves a block of memory of specified size and return a pointer of type void which can be casted into pointer of any form.

Syntax of malloc(): `ptr=(cast-type*)malloc(byte-size)`

Here, ptr is pointer of cast-type. The malloc() function returns a pointer to an area of memory with size of byte size. If the space is insufficient, allocation fails and returns NULL pointer.

For example: `ptr=(int*)malloc(100*sizeof(int));`

This statement will allocate either 200 or 400 according to size of int 2 or 4 bytes respectively and the pointer points to the address of first byte of memory.

2. **calloc():** The name calloc stands for "contiguous allocation". The only difference between malloc() and calloc() is that, malloc() allocates single block of memory whereas calloc() allocates multiple blocks of memory each of same size and sets all bytes to zero.

   Syntax of calloc(): `ptr=(cast-type*)calloc(n,element-size);`

   This statement will allocate contiguous space in memory for an array of n elements.

   For example: `ptr=(float*)calloc(25,sizeof(float));`

   This statement allocates contiguous space in memory for an array of 25 elements each of size of float, i.e, 4 bytes.

3. **free():** Dynamically allocated memory with either calloc() or malloc() does not get return on its own. The programmer must use free() explicitly to release space.

   Syntax of free(): `free(ptr);`

   This statement cause the space in memory pointer by ptr to be deallocated.

Program 4.36: Program to find sum of n elements entered by user. To perform this program, allocate memory dynamically using malloc() function.

```
#include <stdio.h>
#include <stdlib.h>
int main()
{
int n,i,*ptr,sum=0;
printf("Enter number of elements: ");
scanf("%d",&n);
ptr=(int*)malloc(n*sizeof(int)); //memory allocated using malloc
if(ptr==NULL)
{
printf("Error! memory not allocated.");
exit(0);
}
printf("Enter elements of array: ");
```

```c
    for(i=0;i<n;++i)
    {
    scanf("%d",ptr+i);
    sum+=*(ptr+i);
    }
    printf("Sum=%d",sum);
    free(ptr);
    return 0;
    }
```
Output:
```
    Enter number of elements: 4
    Enter elements of array: 1, 2, 4, 6
    Sum = 13
```

Program 4.37: Program to find sum of n elements entered by user. To perform this program, allocate memory dynamically using calloc() function.

```c
    #include <stdio.h>
    #include <stdlib.h>
    int main()
    {
     int n,i,*ptr,sum=0;
     printf("Enter number of elements: ");
     scanf("%d",&n);
     ptr=(int*)calloc(n,sizeof(int));
     if(ptr==NULL)
     {
     printf("Error! memory not allocated.");
     exit(0);
     }
     printf("Enter elements of array: ");
     for(i=0;i<n;++i)
     {
     scanf("%d",ptr+i);
     sum+=*(ptr+i);
     }
     printf("Sum=%d",sum);
     free(ptr);
     return 0;
    }
```
Output:
```
    Enter number of elements: 6
    Enter elements of array: 5 5 6 3 2 4
    Sum = 25
```

4. realloc() function:

- If the previously allocated memory is insufficient or more than sufficient. Then, you can change memory size previously allocated using realloc().
- **Syntax of realloc():** `ptr=realloc(ptr,newsize);`
  Here, ptr is reallocated with size of newsize.

Program 4.38: Program for realloc() function.
```
#include <stdio.h>
#include <stdlib.h>
int main()
{
 int *ptr,i,n1,n2;
 printf("Enter size of array: ");
 scanf("%d",&n1);
 ptr=(int*)malloc(n1*sizeof(int));
 printf("Address of previously allocated memory: ");
 for(i=0;i<n1;++i)
 printf("%u\t",ptr+i);
 printf("\nEnter new size of array: ");
 scanf("%d",&n2);
 ptr=realloc(ptr,n2);
 for(i=0;i<n2;++i)
 printf("%u\t",ptr+i);
 return 0;
}
```
Output:
```
Enter size of array : 2
Address of previously allocated memory: 1894 1896
Enter new size of array : 3
    1894   1896   1898
```

Program 4.39: Program to swap two number using call by reference.
```
#include <stdio.h>
void swap(int *a,int *b);
int main()
{
 int num1=5,num2=10;
 swap(&num1,&num2); /* address of num1 and num2 is passed to swap function */
 printf("Number1 = %d\n",num1);
 printf("Number2 = %d",num2);
 return 0;
}
```

```
void swap(int *a,int *b){ /* pointer a and b points to address of
num1 and num2 respectively */
 int temp;
 temp=*a;
 *a=*b;
 *b=temp;
}
```
Output:
```
Number1 = 10
Number2 = 5
```

Explanation of Program 4.39:
- The address of memory location num1 and num2 are passed to function and the pointers *a and *b accept those values. So, the pointer a and b points to address of num1 and num2 respectively. When, the value of pointer are changed, the value in memory location also changed correspondingly. Hence, change made to *a and *b was reflected in num1 and num2 in main function.

Program 4.40: Program to find largest number using dynamic memory allocation.
```
#include <stdio.h>
#include <stdlib.h>
int main(){
 int i,n;
 float *data;
 printf("Enter total number of elements(1 to 100): ");
 scanf("%d",&n);
 data=(float*)calloc(n,sizeof(float)); /* Allocates the memory for 'n' elements */
 if(data==NULL)
 {
 printf("Error!!! memory not allocated.");
 exit(0);
 }
 printf("\n");
 for(i=0;i<n;++i) /* Stores number entered by user. */
 {
 printf("Enter Number %d: ",i+1);
 scanf("%f",data+i);
 }
```

```
    for(i=1;i<n;++i) /* Loop to store largest number at address data */
    {
    if(*data<*(data+i)) /* Change < to > if you want to find smallest number */
      *data=*(data+i);
    }
    printf("Largest element = %.2f",*data);
    return 0;
    }
```

Output:
```
    Enter total number of elements(1 to 100): 12
    Enter Number 1: 2.34
    Enter Number 2: 3.43
    Enter Number 3: 6.78
    Enter Number 4: 2.45
    Enter Number 5: 7.64
    Enter Number 6: 9.05
    Enter Number 7: -3.45
    Enter Number 8: -9.99
    Enter Number 9: 5.67
    Enter Number 10: 34.953
    Enter Number 11: 4.5
    Enter Number 12: 3.45
    Largest element = 34.95
```

4.10 Functions and Pointers

- The general **syntax for declaring a pointer to a function** is,
  ```
  return-type (*pointer-variable) ();
  ```
- The **general syntax of assignment of a pointer to function** is,
  ```
  pointer-variable = function name;
  ```
- This assigns the address of function i.e. address of the first statement of the function to the pointer-variable.
- The function then can be invoked as `(* pointer-variable) ();`

Program 4.41: Program to illustrate pointer to function.
```
#include<stdio.h>
main()
{
   int display ();
   int (*func_ptr) ();
   func_ptr = display;
/* Assign address of function */
print f ("\n Address of function display is %d", func-ptr);
(*func_ptr) ();
/* invokes function display */
}
int display ()
{
puts ("\n Into the world of pointer to function");
}
```
Output:
```
Address of function display is 679
Into the world of pointer to function
```
- In the above example, func-ptr is a pointer to function which returns an integer. The (*func-ptr) () invokes the function display since func-ptr now points to display.

Program 4.42: Write a program to count the number of words, lines and characters in a text
```
#include<stdio.h>
#include<stdlib.h>
#include<ctype.h>
#include<conio.h>
/*low implies that position of pointer is within a word*/
#define low 1
/*high implies that position of pointer is out of word.*/
#define high 0
void main()
{
int nob,now,nod,nov,nos,pos=high;
char *s;
nob=now=nod=nov=nos=0;
clrscr();
printf("Enter any string:");
gets(s);
```

```c
    while(*s!=' ')
    {
    if(*s==' ') /* counting number of blank spaces. */
     {
     pos=high;
     ++nob;
     }
    else if(pos==high) /* counting number of words. */
     {
     pos=low;
     ++now;
     }
    if(isdigit(*s)) /* counting number of digits. */
     ++nod;
    if(isalpha(*s)) /* counting number of vowels */
     switch(*s)
       {
       case 'a':
       case 'e':
       case 'i':
       case 'o':
       case 'u':
       case 'A':
       case 'E':
       case 'I':
       case 'O':
       case 'U':
       ++nov;
       break;
       }
    /* counting number of special characters */
    if(!isdigit(*s)&&!isalpha(*s))
     ++nos;
    s++;
    }
    printf("\nNumber of words %d",now);
    printf("\nNumber of spaces %d",nob);
    printf("\nNumber of vowels %d",nov);
    printf("\nNumber of digits %d",nod);
    printf("\nNumber of special characters %d",nos);
    getch();
    }
```

Output:
```
Enter any string : NIRALI
Number of words 1
Number of spaces 0
Number of vowels 6
Number of digits 9
Number of special character 228
```

Questions

1. Define function.
2. How to declare a function? Explain with suitable example.
3. State advantages and limitations of function.
4. What is meant by function and recursion.
5. Explain the following parameters passing methods.
   (a) Call by value,
   (b) Call by reference.
6. What is a function? How are the functions declared?
7. Explain the concept of recursion with the help of suitable example.
8. The Fibonacci sequence is given as follows:
   0, 1, 1, 2, 3, 5 ...
   e.g. $F_0 = 0$, $F_1 = 1$, $F_2 = F_0 + F_1$
   $F_n = F_{n-1} + F_{n-2}$.
   Write a recursive function to generate a Fibonacci sequence for a certain number of terms.
9. Write recursive function to convert decimal number into binary number string.
   (For example, 11 → 1011)
10. Write a function to add all even numbers together and add all odd numbers together and print the even sum and odd sum. Accept the number range from the user.
11. Write a function to find out the GCD of 2 given integers.
12. Write a function to check whether the given year (For example: 1999) is a leap year or not. If it is a leap year print "Yes" else print "No".
13. Explain how to return more than one values from a function.
14. What is meant by storage classes?
15. With suitable example explain static storage class.
16. With suitable examples explain auto storage class.
17. With suitable examples explain register storage class.

18. With suitable examples explain extern storage class.
19. Compare auto and static storage class.
20. Define pointer.
21. What is meant by pointer? State its advantages.
22. Enlist various applications of pointers.
23. State advantages and disadvantages of pointer.
24. (a) What will be the output?
    ```
    main( )
    {
        int i;
        * & i = 10;
        printf("%d",i);
    }
    ```
    (b)
    ```
    main( )
    {
        char *p = "aygm";
        char c;
        c = ++ * p++;
        printf("%c",c);
    }
    ```
25. Write a program to reverse the contents of an integer/character array using pointers.
26. Write a program to store a matrix of size m × n using dynamic memory allocation and print the transpose of the matrix.
27. What are pointer variables? How are they different than type of variables? Explain with example.
28. Explain the pointer arithmetic with example.
29. What are pointers to pointers and how are they different from pointers?
30. Write a function with the help of pointers to 'char' to check whether the given string is a palindrome or not.
31. Illustrate the use of pointer to a function by an example.
32. Explain pointer to a function.
33. Write a program illustrating pointer to a function.

■■■

Chapter 5...

Arrays and Strings

Contents ...

5.1 Introduction to Arrays
5.2 One-dimensional Array
    5.2.1 Definition
    5.2.2 Declaration
    5.2.3 Initialization
5.3 Two-dimensional Array
    5.3.1 Definition
    5.3.2 Declaration and Initialization
5.4 Arrays and Functions
5.5 Introduction to String
    5.5.1 Definition
    5.5.2 Declaration and Initialization
5.6 String Functions
    5.6.1 String Character related Functions
    5.6.2 Standard Library Functions
5.7 Implementation without Standard Library Functions
- Questions

5.1 Introduction to Arrays

- An array is a collection of variables of the same data type and it is referenced by a common name.
- An array is a linear and homogeneous data structure.
- Linear data structure stores its individual data elements in a sequential order in the memory. Homogeneous means all individual data elements are of the same data type.
- An array is a group of data items of the same data type which share a common name.
- An array should be of a single type, comprising of integers or strings.
- All arrays consist of contiguous memory locations. The lowest address corresponds to the first element and the highest address to the last element.

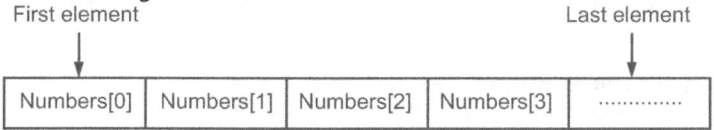

Fig. 5.1: Array and its elements

Definition of Array:
- Array is a collection of variables belongings to the same data type.

OR

- We can define array as "a variable that hold multiple elements which has the same data type".

OR

- An array is a sequence of data item of homogeneous value (same type).
- Various **properties** of arrays are:
  1. The size of an array is the number of elements in each dimension.
  2. The number of dimensions.
  3. The type of an array is the data type of its elements.
  4. The name of an array.

Declaration of an Array:
- Array is a collection of homogenous data stored under unique name.
- The values in an array is called as 'elements of an array.' These elements are accessed by numbers called as 'subscripts or index numbers.'
- Arrays may be of any variable type.
- Array is also called as 'subscripted variable.'
- An array is declared as,

data_type name_of_array [size];

Program 5.1: Program for displaying value entered by user.

```
#include<stdio.h>
void main()
{
   int value[5], i;
   for(i=0;i<5;i++)
   {
    printf("Enter value: ");
    scanf("%d", &value[]);
    printf("\n");
   }
   for(i=0;i<5;i++)
   {
    printf("Value = %d\n", value[i]);
    getch();
   }
}
```

Output:
```
Enter value : 0
Enter value : 1
Enter value : 2
Enter value : 3
Enter value : 4
Value = 0
Value = 1
Value = 2
Value = 3
Value = 4
```
- Here, each value entered by the user will be overwritten in the variable value. So, finally the last value '5' will be stored in value and it will get printed 5 times. So, we have to make use of an array to store 5 different integer values.

Accessing Array Elements and Displaying Array Elements:
- An element is accessed by indexing the array name. This is done by placing the index of the element within square brackets after the name of the array.
- For example:
    ```
    double salary = balance[9];
    ```
- The above statement will be take 10th elements from the array and assign the value of salary variable.

Program 5.2: Program for array.
```c
#include <stdio.h>
int main ()
{
  int n[ 10 ]; /* n is an array of 10 integers */
  int i,j;
  /* initialize elements of array n to 0 */
  for ( i = 0; i < 10; i++ )
  {
  n[ i ] = i + 100; /* set element at location i to i + 100 */
  }
  /* output each array element's value */
  for (j = 0; j < 10; j++ )
  {
  printf("Element[%d] = %d\n", j, n[j] );
  }
  return 0;
}
```

Output:
```
Element[0] = 100
Element[1] = 101
Element[2] = 102
Element[3] = 103
Element[4] = 104
Element[5] = 105
Element[6] = 106
Element[7] = 107
Element[8] = 108
Element[9] = 109
```

Program 5.3: Program for sum of values in an array.
```
#include<stdio.h>
void main()
{
  int i, numbers[10] = {4, 8, 2, -11, 4, 5, 3, 33, -28, 65};
  for (i=0,numbers[10]=0; i<10; i++)
  {
  numbers[10] = numbers[i] + numbers[10];
printf("Sum of values of array, numbers[10]= %d\n",numbers[10]);
  }
}
```

Output:
```
Sum of values of array, numbers[10] = 4
Sum of values of array, numbers[10] = 12
Sum of values of array, numbers[10] = 14
Sum of values of array, numbers[10] = 3
Sum of values of array, numbers[10] = 7
Sum of values of array, numbers[10] = 12
Sum of values of array, numbers[10] = 15
Sum of values of array, numbers[10] = 48
Sum of values of array, numbers[10] = 20
Sum of values of array, numbers[10] = 85
```

Program 5.4: Program for Fibonacci Series.

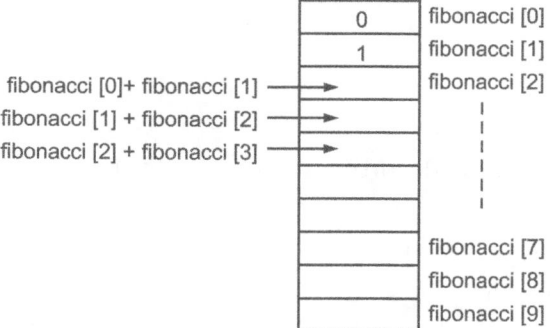

Fig. 5.2

```
#include<stdio.h>
void main()
{
    int i, n, fibonacci[30];
    clrscr();
    printf("Enter the number of values you want: ");
    scanf("%d",&n);
    fibonacci[0] = 0;
    fibonacci[1] = 1;
    for(i=2;i<n;i++)
        fibonacci[i] = fibonacci[i-1] + fibonacci[i-2];
    printf("Fibonacci Series - \n");
     for(i=0;i<n;i++)
        printf("%d\n", fibonacci[i]);
}
```

Output:

```
Enter the number of values you want: 5
Fibonacci series-
0
1
1
2
3
```

Program 5.5: Program to find maximum number.
```
#include<stdio.h>
void main()
{
   int i, num[10], max;
   printf("Enter any 10 integer values: \n");
   for(i=0;i<10;i++)
      scanf("%d",&num[i]);
   for(i=0;i<10;i++)
   {
      if (num[i] > num[i + 1])
         num[i+1] = num[i];
   }
   printf("The maximum number of the given 10 numbers is %d \n", num[9]);
}
```
Output:
```
Enter any 10 integer value:
1
3
5
8
15
14
11
12
13
2
The maximum number of the given 10 numbers is 15
```

Program 5.6: Program to find largest element of an array.
```
#include <stdio.h>
int main()
{
int i,n;
float arr[100];
printf("Enter total number of elements(1 to 100): ");
scanf("%d",&n);
printf("\n");
```

```c
    for(i=0;i<n;++i) /* Stores number entered by user. */
    {
      printf("Enter Number %d: ",i+1);
      scanf("%f",&arr[i]);
    }
    for(i=1;i<n;++i) /* Loop to store largest number to arr[0] */
    {
      if(arr[0]<arr[i]) /* Change < to > if you want to find smallest element*/
      arr[0]=arr[i];
    }
    printf("Largest element = %.2f",arr[0]);
    return 0;
    }
```

Output:
```
Enter total number of elements(1 to 100): 12
Enter Number 1: 2.34
Enter Number 2: 3.43
Enter Number 3: 6.78
Enter Number 4: 2.45
Enter Number 5: 7.64
Enter Number 6: 9.05
Enter Number 7: -3.45
Enter Number 8: -9.99
Enter Number 9: 5.67
Enter Number 10: 34.953
Enter Number 11: 4.5
Enter Number 12: 3.45
Largest element = 34.95
```

Program 5.7: Program to calculate average using arrays.

```c
    #include <stdio.h>
    int main()
    {
    int n, i;
    float num[100], sum=0.0, average;
    printf("Enter the numbers of data: ");
    scanf("%d",&n);
```

```c
while (n>100 || n<=0)
{
printf("Error! number should in range of (1 to 100).\n");
printf("Enter the number again: ");
scanf("%d",&n);
}
for(i=0; i<n; ++i)
{
printf("%d. Enter number: ",i+1);
scanf("%f",&num[i]);
sum+=num[i];
}
average=sum/n;
printf("Average = %.2f",average);
return 0;
}
```

Output:
```
Enter the total numbers of data: 141
Error! number should in range of (1 to 100).
Enter the number again: 9
1. Enter Number: 12.34
2. Enter Number: 45.678
3. Enter Number: -3.45
4. Enter Number: 0
5. Enter Number: 33.48
6. Enter Number: -234.53
7. Enter Number: 111.11
8. Enter Number: 222.432
9. Enter Number: 43.45
Average = 25.61
```

Advantages of Arrays:
1. Easy to use.
2. Any element in an array can be accessed immediately (random access) if its exact position in the array is known.

Disadvantages of arrays are given below:
1. Elements cannot be inserted into an array.
2. Arrays do not support copy assignment.
3. Constant data type.
4. Constant size.
5. Large free sequential block to accommodate large arrays.

5.2 One-dimensional Array

- The array which is used to represent and store data in a linear form is called as 'single or one dimensional array.
- The arrays seen so far can be represented as a row or as a column. In other words, it can be represented as in a single dimension-width or height.

5.2.1 Definition

- An array which is having either a single row or single column is termed as a one-dimensional array. One dimensional array have the subscripts in a linear manner.

OR

- Single / One Dimensional Array is an array having a single index value to represent the arrays element.

OR

- The array which is used to represent and store data in a linear form is called as 'single or one dimensional array.'
- Fig. 5.3 shows a single dimension array or a 1D array, represented row-wise or column-wise. Such 1D arrays are also called as linear lists.

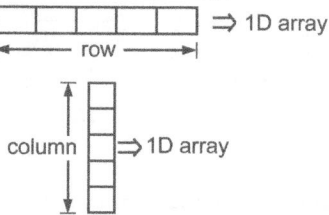

Fig. 5.3: One-dimensional array

- Now, consider a student marklist is to be maintained, specifying roll no of each student and their respective marks. In such case, we will require a 1D array for student roll no and 1D arrays for their respective subject marks. It is pretty difficult to work on such n arrays.

5.2.2 Declaration

- One-dimensional array also called as linear list, the syntax for declaration of one-dimensional array is given below.
- **Syntax** of single dimesional array are:

    <data_type> <array_name> [size];

    Where,

datatype	:	The type of the data stores in the array.
arrayname	:	Name of the array.
size	:	Maximum number of elements that an array can hold.

Example: int marks [1 2]

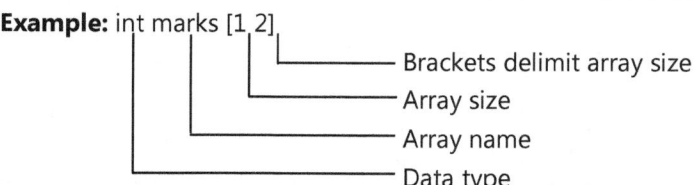

- Above example represents the marks of the 12 students.
- In this example, we are representing a set of 12 student marks and the computer allocates 11 storage locations as shown below:

Marks of the 12th student

| mark[0] | mark[1] | ... | mark[11] |

Example:
```
int a[3] = {2, 3, 5};
char ch[20] = "TechnoExam";
float stax[3] = {5003.23, 1940.32, 123.20};
```
Total Size (in Bytes):
```
total size = length of array * size of data type
```
- In above example, a is an array of type integer which has storage size of 3 elements. The total size would be 3 * 2 = 6 bytes.
- **Memory Allocation:**

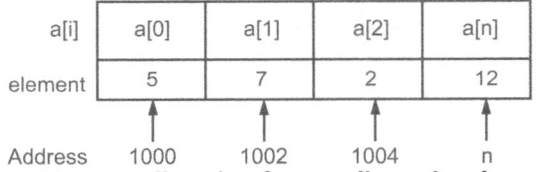

Fig. 5.4: Memory allocation for one dimensional array

Program 5.8: Program to demonstrate one dimensional array.
```
#include<stdio.h>
#include<conio.h>
void main()
{
   int a[3], i;;
   clrscr();
   printf("\n\t Enter three numbers: ");
   for(i=0; i<3; i++)
   {
      scanf("%d", &a[i]); // read array
   }
   printf("\n\n\t Numbers are: ");
   for(i=0; i<3; i++)
   {
      printf("\t %d", a[i]); // print array
   }
   getch();
}
```
Output:
```
Enter three numbers: 9 4 6
Numbers are: 9 4 6
```

Program 5.9: Program for 1D array.
```
#include<stdio.h>
#include<conio.h>
int main()
{
   int i, numbers[5];
   clrscr();
   printf("Enter five numbers \n");
   for(i=0; i<5; i++)
   scanf("%d", &numbers[i]);
   printf("Array elements are \n");
   for(i=0; i<5; i++)
   printf("%d \n", numbers[i]);
   getch();
   return 0;
}
```
Output:
```
Enter five numbers
4
6
7
3
2
Array elements are:
4
6
7
3
2
```
Features:
1. Array size should be positive number only.
2. String array always terminates with null character ('\0').
3. Array elements are countered from 0 to n-1.
4. Useful for multiple reading of elements (numbers).

Disadvantages of one-dimensional array:
1. There is no easy method to initialize large number of array elements.
2. It is difficult to initialize selected elements.

5.2.3 Initialization

- User can initialize the array element one by one.
  Syntax: `array_name[index] = value;`
  Example: `mark[0] = 40;`
  `mark[1] = 90;`
  ....
  ....
  `mark[11] = 91`

- User can also initialize the complete array directly as:
  Syntax: `type arrayname[] = {list of values};`
  Example: `int mark[12] = {40, 90, 27, 20, 43, 56, 82, 78, 86, 80, 91};`

- This array is stored in the memory as follows:

40	90	42	57	20	43	56	82	78	86	80	91
mark[0]	mark[1]	mark[2]	mark[3]	mark[4]	mark[5]	mark[6]	mark[7]	mark[8]	mark[9]	mark[10]	mark[11]

  Example: `char a[8] = {'P', 'R', 'A', 'G', 'A', 'T', 'I'};`
- This array is stored in the memory as follows:

'P'	'R'	'A'	'G'	'A'	'T'	'I'	'\0'
a[0]	a[1]	a[2]	a[3]	a[4]	a[5]	a[6]	a[7]

- When the compiler sees a character array, it terminates it with an additional null character. When declaring character arrays, we must always allow one extra element space for the null terminator.
- The declaration and initialization of float array:
  Example: `float price[4] = {2, 0.50, 4.00, 10.4};`
- This array is stored in the memory as follows:

2.25	0.50	4.00	10.4
price[0]	price[1]	price[2]	price[3]

- Symbolic constants may also appear in array declarations:
  Example: `#define qty 12`
  `int item[qty]; // declares items as an array of 12 elements.`

5.3 Two-dimensional Array

- The array which is used to represent and store data in a tabular form is called as 'two dimensional array.' Such type of array specially used to represent data in a matrix form.

5.3.1 Definition

- Two Dimensional Array is a simple form of multi-dimensional array that stores the array elements in a row, column matrix format.

OR

- Two-dimensional array are those type of array, which has finite number of rows and finite number of columns.

- The other option is to have a single array with 2-dimension (rows and columns), which will store all the information as shown in the Fig. 5.5.

	column 0	column 1	....	column n
	Subject Roll no	Maths	Computer		
row 0	4001	......	......	......	......
row 1	4002	......	......	......	......
:	:	......	......	......	......
:	:	......	......	......	......
row n	:	......	......	......	......

Fig. 5.5: Two-dimensional array

- Here, row consists of student roll no and column consists of subjects. So, the total items in this array would be,

$$rows \times columns$$

- A two dimensional array is referred as a matrix or a table.
- A matrix has two subscripts, one denotes the row and the other denotes the column. The first dimension (i.e. the first index) might refer to the row number, and the second dimension (i.e. the second index) to the column number.
- The general declaration of a 2D array is given as,

    type name[row] [column];

    where, type, specifies data type of the array

    name, specifies name of the array

    row, specifies number of rows in the array

    column, specifies number of columns in the array

- So, an array by the name 'value' of character data type having 3 rows and 1 column will be declared as,

    char value[3][1]

- Now, a step further. To enter the values into a 2D array, we require nested for loops. The inner for loop indicates the column number, while the outer for loop indicates the row number.
- The rows are represented starting from 0 to n. The columns are represented starting from 0 to m. The size of the array, with n rows and m columns is given as n × m.

5.3.2 Declaration and Initialization

1. **Two-dimensional Array Declaration:**

    Syntax: data_type array_name[rows] [columns];

Where,

    data_type   :   The type of the data stored in the array
    array_name   :   Name of the array
    rows   :   Maximum number of rows in the array
    columns   :   Maximum number of columns in the array

Example   : `int value[3] [3];`   // implies 3 rows and 3 columns

2. **Initialization of Two Dimensional Array:**

    `int table[2] [3] = {2, 11, 3, 5, 1, 10};`

- Above initialized two-dimensional array can be stored in the memory in any of the three foms mentioned below:

1. Two-dimensional form as follows:

	col 0	col 1	col 2
row 0	2	11	3
row 1	5	1	10

2. **Row-wise linear list:** Elements of row0 are stored first and then row1 is stored.

table[0] [0]	table[0] [1]	table[0] [2]	table [1] [0]	table [1] [1]	table [1] [2]
2	11	3	5	1	10

                row0   row1

3. **Column-wise linear list:** Elements of col0 are stored first, next col1 and next col2.

table[0] [0]	table[0] [1]	table[0] [2]	table [1] [0]	table [1] [1]	table [1] [2]
2	5	11	1	3	10

            col0   col1   col2

Example:

    `int a[3][3];`

In above example, a is an array of type integer which has storage size of 3 * 3 matrix. The total size would be 3 * 3 * 2 = 18 bytes. It is also called as 'multidimensional array.'

- **Memory Allocation:**

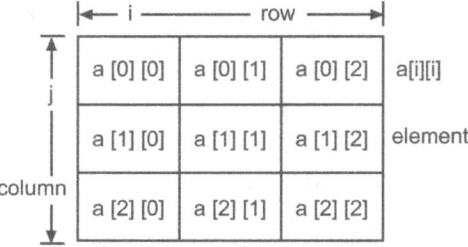

Fig. 5.6: Memory allocation for two dimensional array

Program 5.10: Program to demonstrate two dimensional array.
```
#include<stdio.h>
#include<conio.h>
void main()
{
   int a[3][3], i, j;
   clrscr();
   printf("\n\t Enter matrix of 3*3: ");
   for(i=0; i<3; i++)
   {
      for(j=0; j<3; j++)
      {
      scanf("%d",&a[i][j]); //read 3*3 array
      }
   }
   printf("\n\t Matrix is: \n");
   for(i=0; i<3; i++)
   {
      for(j=0; j<3; j++)
      {
      printf("\t %d",a[i][j]); //print 3*3 array
      }
    printf("\n");
   }
   getch();
}
```
Output:
```
   Enter matrix of 3*3: 3 4 5 6 7 2 1 2 3

   Matrix is:
   3   4   5
   6   7   2
   1   2   3
```

- **Limitations of two dimensional array:**
  1. We cannot delete any element from an array.
  2. If we don't know that how many elements have to be stored in a memory in advance, then there will be memory wastage if large array size is specified.

Program 5.11: Program for two dimensional array.

```
#include<stdio.h>
#include<conio.h>
int main()
{
    int matrix[3][3],i,j,r,c;
    clrscr();
    printf("Enter the order of matrix \n');
    scanf("%d%d",&r,&c);
    printf("Entger elements of %d * %d matrix \n",r,c);
    for(i=0;i<r;i++)
        for(j=0;j<c;j++)
            scanf("%d",&matrix[i][j]);
    printf("Given matrix:\n");
    for(i=0;i<r;i++)
    {
    for(j=0;j<c;j++)
    printf("%d\t",matrix[i][j]);
    printf("\n");
    }
    printf("\t",matrix[2][2]);
    getch();
    return 0;
}
```

Output:
```
Enter the order of matrix
2
2
Enter elements of 2*2 matrix
1
2
3
4
Given matrix:
1  2
3  4
```

Program 5.12: Program for sum of individual elements of 2D array.
```c
#include<stdio.h>
void main()
{
    int i, j, sum;
    int elements[3][7]  = { {0, 2, 4, 6, 8, 10, 12} ,
                            {14, 16, 18, 20, 22, 24, 26},
                            {28, 30, 32, 34, 36, 38, 40} };
    clrscr();
    for(i=0,sum=0;i<3;i++)
    {
       for(j=0;j<7;j++)
            sum = sum + elements[i][j];
    }
    printf("The result of addition = %d \n", sum);
}
```
Output:
```
The result of addition = 420
```

Program 5.13: Program for displaying marks of students.
```c
#include<stdio.h>
void main()
{
    int i, j;
    int marks[3][5]   = {{65, 68, 75, 59, 77},
                         {62, 85, 57, 66, 80},
                         {71, 77, 66, 63, 86} };
    float avg;
    printf("\n\t\t");
    for(i=0;i<5;i++)
    printf("subj%d\t",i+1);
    printf("\n");
    for(i=0;i<3;i++)
    {
      printf("student%d\t",i+1);
      for(j=0;j<5;j++)
      printf("%d\t",marks[i][j]);
      printf("\n");
    }
```

```c
        printf("\n\nThe Average of each subject is: \n");
        for(j=0;j<5;j++)
        {
           printf("Subject%d: ",j+1);
           for(i=0,avg=0;i<3;i++)
           avg = avg + (float)marks[i][j];
           avg = avg / 3;
           printf("%.2f\n", avg);
        }
        getch();
    }
```

Output:

```
The Average of each subject is:
Subject 1 : 66.00
Subject 2 : 76.67
Subject 3 : 66.00
Subject 4 : 62.67
Subject 5 : 81.00
```

Multi-dimensional array:
- Arrays can have more than one dimension, these arrays-of-arrays are called multidimensional arrays.
- They are very similar to standard arrays with the exception that they have multiple sets of square brackets after the array identifier.

Definition:
- An array with more than one index value is called a multidimensional array.

OR

- Arrays can have more than one dimension, these arrays-of-arrays are called multidimensional arrays.
- They are very similar to standard arrays with the exception that they have multiple sets of square brackets after the array identifier. A two dimensional array can be though of as a grid of rows and columns.
- C supports multidimensional arrays. Arrays can have higher dimensions.
- Two-dimensional arrays are identified by two subscripts, three-dimensionals arrays have three subscripts and so on.
- In general, an n-dimensional array declaration is as shown below:

    < data type > array name [n] [m] ……

Program 5.14: Program for multidimensional array.
```
#include<stdio.h>
const int num_rows = 7;
const int num_columns = 5;
int main()
{
int box[num_rows][num_columns];
int row, column;
for(row = 0; row < num_rows; row++)
for(column = 0; column < num_columns; column++)
box[row][column] = column + (row * num_columns);
for(row = 0; row < num_rows; row++)
{
for(column = 0; column < num_columns; column++)
{
printf("%4d", box[row][column]);
}
printf("\n");
}
return 0;
}
```
Output:
```
   0   1   2   3   4
   5   6   7   8   9
  10  11  12  13  14
  15  16  17  18  19
  20  21  22  23  24
  25  26  27  28  29
  30  31  32  33  34
```

Program 5.15: Program to find sum of two matrix of order 2*2 using multidimensional arrays where, elements of matrix are entered by user.
```
#include <stdio.h>
int main()
{
float a[2][2], b[2][2], c[2][2];
int i,j;
printf("Enter the elements of 1st matrix\n");
```

```c
/* Reading two dimensional Array with the help of two for loop. If
there was an array of 'n' dimension, 'n' numbers of loops are needed
for inserting data to array.*/
for(i=0;i<2;++i)
for(j=0;j<2;++j)
{
printf("Enter a%d%d: ",i+1,j+1);
scanf("%f",&a[i][j]);
}
printf("Enter the elements of 2nd matrix\n");
for(i=0;i<2;++i)
for(j=0;j<2;++j)
{
printf("Enter b%d%d: ",i+1,j+1);
scanf("%f",&b[i][j]);
}
for(i=0;i<2;++i)
for(j=0;j<2;++j){
/* Writing the elements of multidimensional array using loop. */
c[i][j]=a[i][j]+b[i][j]; /* Sum of corresponding elements of two
arrays. */
}
printf("\nSum Of Matrix:\n");
for(i=0;i<2;++i)
for(j=0;j<2;++j)
{
printf("%.1f\t",c[i][j]);
if(j==1) /* To display matrix sum in order. */
printf("\n");
}
return 0;
}
```

Output:
```
Enter the elements of 1st matrix
Enter a11: 2;
Enter a12: 0.5;
Enter a21: -1.1;
Enter a22: 2;
Enter the elements of 2nd matrix
Enter a11: 0.2;
Enter a12: 0;
Enter a21: 0.23;
Enter b22: 23;
Sum of Matrix:

2.2    0.5
-0.9   25.0
```

5.4 Arrays and Functions

- Arrays can be used within different functions or they can be called and passed to and from from different functions.
- Array can be passed to a function in two way one is element by element and another is passing the entire array.

Program 5.16: Program for display 0-5 integers using functions.

```
#include<stdio.h>
void main()
{
   void display ();
   printf("First Six Integers:\n");
   display ();
}
   void display ()
   {
   int i, num[10] = {0, 1, 2, 3, 4, 5};
   for (i=0; i<6; i++)
   {
      printf("%d\n",num[i]);
   }
}
```

Output:
```
First Six Integers
0
1
2
3
4
5
```

1. **Passing the array element by element:**

   In these method the array element can be passed one-by-one to the function. The function gets access for only one element at a time and cannot modify the value.

   For example:
   ```
   #include<stdio.h>
   #include<conio.h>
   main()
   {
    int a[3] = {10, 20, 30};
    void display(int);
    int i;
    for (i=0; i<3; i++)
    display(a[i];
   }
    void display(int b)
    {
       printf("%d", b);
    }
   ```

2. **Passing the entire array:**
   In these method we just have to send the name of the array to the function.
   For example:
   ```
   #include<stdio.h>
   #include<conio.h>
   main()
   {
    int a[3] = {10, 20, 30};
    void modify(int x[3]);
    modify (a);
   {
    void modify (int x[3])
    {
        int i;
        for(i=0; i<3; i++)
        x[i] = x[i] * 3;
   }
   ```

- One of the most important operation of array is sorting. Sorting means arranging the array element is either ascending or descending order.

Program 5.17: Program for sorting of array (ascending order).
```
#include<stdio.h>
void main()
{
    int i, j, temp;
    int ascend[10];
    printf("Enter the 10 integer values to be sorted-\n");
    for(i=0;i<10;i++)
    {
        scanf("%d",&ascend[i]);
    printf("Original Array -\n\n");
    }
    for(i=0;i<10;i++)
        {
        printf("%d\t",ascend[i]);
        }
```

```c
        for(i=0;i<9;i++)
        {
            for(j=i+1;j<10;j++)
            {
                if (ascend[i] > ascend[j])
                {
                    temp = ascend[i];
                    ascend[i] = ascend[j];
                    ascend[j] = temp;
                }
            }
        }
        printf("\nSorted Array - \n\n");
        for(i=0;i<10;i++)
        {
            printf("%d\t",ascend[i]);
        }
    }
```

Output:
```
Enter the 10 integer values to be sorted -
3   6   13   -10   33  23 6   9   5   40
Sorted Array -
-10   3   5   6     6   9   13   23  33  40
```

Program 5.18: Sorting an array in descending order.

```c
    #include<stdio.h>
    int i, j, temp;
    int descend[10];
    void main()
    {
        void descending ();
        printf("Enter the 10 integer values to be sorted - \n");
        for(i=0;i<10;i++)
        {
        scanf("%d",&descend[i]);
        printf("Original Array - \n\n");
        }
```

```c
    for(i=0;i<10;i++)
    {
    printf("%d\t",descend[i]);
    }
    descending ();
    printf("\nSorted Array - \n\n");
    for(i=0;i<10;i++)
    printf("%d\t",descend[i]);
    getch();
}
void descending ()
{
    for(i=0;i<9;i++)
    {
        for (j=i+1; j<10; j++)
        {
            if (descend[i] < descend [j])
            {
                temp = descend[i];
                descend[i] = descend[j];
                descend[j] = temp;
            }
        }
    }
}
```

Output:
```
Enter the 10 integer values to be sorted:
Original Array
     1
Original Array
     2
Original Array
     3
Original Array
     4
Original Array
     5
Original Array
     6
Original Array
     7
Original Array
     8
Original Array
     9
Original Array
     10
Sorted Array
10   9   8   7   6   5 4   3   2   1
```

Programs on Arrays

Program 1: Write a program to print contents of array which is initialized.

```
#include<stdio.h>
void main()
{
    int array[5] = { 23, 17, 39, 92, 18};
    int i;
    clrscr();
        for(i=0;i<5;i++)
    {
            printf("\n %d", array[i]);
    }
    getch();
}
```
Output:
```
23
17
39
92
18
```

Program 2: Write a program to store the elements in the array and to print them from the array.

```
#include<stdio.h>
#include<conio.h>
void main()
{
    int array[5],i;
    printf("\n Enter 5 numbers to store them in array \n");
    for(i=0;i<5;i++)
    {
        scanf("%d",&array[i]);
    }
    printf("Element in the array are - \n \n");
    for(i=0;i<5;i++)
    {
        printf("\n Element stored at a[%d] = %d \n",i,array[i]);
    }
    getch();
}
```

Output:
```
Enter 5 numbers to store them in array
   23 56 17 98 22
Element in the array are-
Element stored at a[0] = 23
Element stored at a[1] = 56
Element stored at a[2] = 17
Element stored at a[3] = 98
Element stored at a[4] = 22
```

Program 3: Write a program to Input 10 numbers from user and find the total of all of them.

```c
#include<stdio.h>
#include<conio.h>
void main( )
{
   int val[10], i, total=0;
   printf("Enter any ten numbers: ");
   for(i=0;i<10;i++)
   {
     scanf("%d", &val[i]);           // input numbers
   }
   for(i=0;i<10;i++)
   {
     total = total + val[i];         // find total
   }
   printf("\nTotal is: %d", total);
}
```

Output:
```
Enter any ten numbers: 10 20 30 40 50 60 70 80 90 100
Total is: 550
```

Program 4: Write a program to count the number of positive negative and zeros from given one dimensional array of n elements?

```c
#include<stdio.h>
#include<conio.h>
#define size 15
void main()
{
int input[size],i,neg=0,pos=0,zro=0;n;
clrscr();
```

```c
printf("how many elements you want enter(should be less than
%d:",size);
scanf("%d",&n);
printf("enter elements into array:\n");
for(i=0;i<n;i++)
scanf("%d",&input[i]);
for(i=0;i<n;i++)
{
   if(input[i]>0)
   pos++;
   if(input[i]<0)
   neg++;
   if(input[i]==0)
   zro++;
}
printf("number of positive elements:%d\n",pos);
printf("number of negetive elements:%d\n",neg);
printf("number of zero elements:%d\n",zro);
getch();
}
```

Output:
```
How many elements you want enter(should be less than 15)
8
enter elements into array:
4 -8 7 13 -23 0 45 0
number of positive elements:4
number of negative elements:2
number of zero elements:2
```

Program 5: Write a program to find the smallest and largest number from an array.
```c
#include<stdio.h>
#include<conio.h>
void main()
{
int a[10],n,i,large,small;
printf("enter the number of elements :\n");
scanf("%d",&n);
printf("enter the elements :\n");
```

```
    for(i=0;i<n;i++)
    scanf("%d",&a[i]);
    large=a[0];
    small=a[0];
    for(i=1;i<n;i++)
    {
       if(a[i]>large)
       large=a[i];
       if(a[i]<small);
       small=a[i];
    }
    printf("largest element in the array is : %d\n",large);
    printf("smallest element in the array is : %d\n",small);
    getch();
    }
```

Output:
```
    enter the number of elements : 5
    enter the elements :
    78
    23
    7
    19
    35
    largest element in the array is : 78
    smallest element in the array is : 7
```

Program 6: Write a program to initialized two dimensional array and print the contents.

```
    #include<stdio.h>
    void main()
    {
    int j, array[2][2] = {
                {10,20},
                {30,40}
          };
    int i=j=0;
    clrscr();
    printf("\n Array contents are :");
```

```c
    for(i=0;i<2;i++)
    {
        for(j=0;j<2;j++)
        {
          printf("%d", array[i][j]);
        }
        printf("\n");
    }
    getch();
    }
```
Output:
```
Array contents are :
10 20
30 40
```

Program 7: Write a program to accept elements for the matrix and display the contents.
```c
    #include <stdio.h>
    #include <conio.h>
    void main()
    {
       int a[3][3], i, j;
       clrscr();
       printf("\n\t Enter matrix of 3*3 : ");
       for(i=0; i<3; i++)
       {
         for(j=0; j<3; j++)
         {
         scanf("%d",&a[i][j]);   //read 3*3 array
         }
       }
       printf("\n\t Matrix is : \n");
       for(i=0; i<3; i++)
       {
         for(j=0; j<3; j++)
         {
         printf("\t %d",a[i][j]);   //print 3*3 array
         }
           printf("\n");
       }
       getch();
    }
```

Output:
```
Enter matrix of 3*3 : 2 3 6 9 4 1 5 7 8
Matrix is :
2   3   6
9   4   1
5   7   8
```

Program 8: Write a program to perform addition of two 3*3 matrix.

```c
/*Addition of two matrix*/
#include<stdio.h>
#include<conio.h>
void main()
{
   int x[][] = { {8,5,6},
       {1,2,1},
       {0,8,7}
            };
   int y[][] = {  {4,3,2},
       {3,6,4},
       {0,0,0}
            };
   int i,j;
   printf("First matrix:\n");
   for(i=0;i<3;i++)
   {
     for(j=0;j<3;j++)
       printf("%d", x[i][j]);
       printf("\n");
   }
   printf("Second matrix:\n");
   for(i=0;i<3;i++)
   {
     for(int j=0;j<3;j++)
       printf("%d   ", y[i][j]);
       printf("\n");
   }
   printf("Addition:\n");
```

```
    for(i=0;i<3;i++)
    {
      for(int j=0;j<3;j++)
        printf("%d   ", x[i][j]+y[i][j]);
        printf("\n");
    }
    getch();
}
```

Output

```
First matrix:
8  5  6
1  2  1
0  8  7
Second matrix:
4  3  2
3  6  4
0  0  0
Addition:
12 8  8
4  8  5
0  8  7
```

Program 9: Program to reverse an array.

C program to reverse an array: This program reverses the array elements. For example if a is an array of integers with three elements such that

a[0] = 1
a[1] = 2
a[2] = 3

Then on reversing the array will be,

a[0] = 3
a[1] = 2
a[0] = 1

```c
#include <stdio.h>
int main()
{
int n, c, d, a[100], b[100];
printf("Enter the number of elements in array\n");
scanf("%d", &n);
printf("Enter the array elements\n");
```

```c
    for (c = 0; c < n ; c++)
    scanf("%d", &a[c]);
    /*
     * Copying elements into array b starting from end of array a
     */
    for (c = n - 1, d = 0; c >= 0; c--, d++)
    b[d] = a[c];
    /*
     * Copying reversed array into original.
     * Here we are modifying original array, this is optional.
     */
    for (c = 0; c < n; c++)
    a[c] = b[c];
    printf("Reverse array is\n");
    for (c = 0; c < n; c++)
    printf("%d\n", a[c]);
    return 0;
    }
```

Output:

```
Enter the number of elements in array
5
Enter the array elements
4
8
45
4568
1231
Reverse array is
1231
4568
45
8
4
```

Program 10: Program to insert an element in an array.
- This code will insert an element into an array, For example consider an array a[10] having three elements in it initially and a[0] = 1, a[1] = 2 and a[2] = 3 and you want to insert a number 45 at location 1 i.e. a[0] = 45, so we have to move elements one step below so after insertion a[1] = 1 which was a[0] initially, and a[2] = 2 and a[3] = 3. Array insertion does not mean increasing its size i.e array will not be containing 11 elements.

```c
#include <stdio.h>
int main()
{
  int array[100], position, c, n, value;
  printf("Enter number of elements in array\n");
  scanf("%d", &n);
  printf("Enter %d elements\n", n);
  for (c = 0; c < n; c++)
  scanf("%d", &array[c]);
  printf("Enter the location where you wish to insert an element\n");
  scanf("%d", &position);
  printf("Enter the value to insert\n");
  scanf("%d", &value);
  for (c = n - 1; c >= position - 1; c--)
  array[c+1] = array[c];
  array[position-1] = value;
  printf("Resultant array is\n");
  for (c = 0; c <= n; c++)
  printf("%d\n", array[c]);
  return 0;
}
```

Output:
```
Enter the number of elements in array
5
Enter 5 elements
2
5
4
3
8
Enter the location where you wish to insert an element
4
Enter the value to insert
10
Resultant array is
2
5
4
10
3
8
```

Program 11: Program to delete an element from an array.
```c
#include <stdio.h>
int main()
{
 int array[100], position, c, n;
 printf("Enter number of elements in array\n");
 scanf("%d", &n);
 printf("Enter %d elements\n", n);
 for ( c = 0 ; c < n ; c++ )
 scanf("%d", &array[c]);
 printf("Enter the location where you wish to delete element\n");
 scanf("%d", &position);
 if ( position >= n+1 )
 printf("Deletion not possible.\n");
 else
 {
 for ( c = position - 1 ; c < n - 1 ; c++ )
 array[c] = array[c+1];
 printf("Resultant array is\n");
 for( c = 0 ; c < n - 1 ; c++ )
 printf("%d\n", array[c]);
 }
 return 0;
}
```
Output:
```
Enter number of elements in array
5
Enter 5 elements
4
6
8
10
7
Enter the location where you wish to delete element
2
Resultant array is
4
8
10
7
```

Program 12: Program to merge two arrays.
```c
#include <stdio.h>
void merge(int [], int, int [], int, int []);
int main() {
 int a[100], b[100], m, n, c, sorted[200];
 printf("Input number of elements in first array\n");
 scanf("%d", &m);
 printf("Input %d integers\n", m);
 for (c = 0; c < m; c++)
 {
 scanf("%d", &a[c]);
 }
 printf("Input number of elements in second array\n");
 scanf("%d", &n);
 printf("Input %d integers\n", n);
 for (c = 0; c < n; c++)
 {
 scanf("%d", &b[c]);
 }
 merge(a, m, b, n, sorted);
 printf("Sorted array:\n");
 for (c = 0; c < m + n; c++)
 {
 printf("%d\n", sorted[c]);
 }
 return 0;
}
void merge(int a[], int m, int b[], int n, int sorted[]) {
 int i, j, k;
 j = k = 0;
 for (i = 0; i < m + n;)
 {
 if (j < m && k < n)
 {
 if (a[j] < b[k])
 {
 sorted[i] = a[j];
 j++;
 }
```

```
      else {
      sorted[i] = b[k];
      k++;
      }
      i++;
      }
      else if (j == m)
     {
      for (; i < m + n;)
     {
      sorted[i] = b[k];
      k++;
      i++;
      }
     }
      else
     {
      for (; i < m + n;)
     {
      sorted[i] = a[j];
      j++;
      i++;
      }
     }
    }
}
```

Output:
```
Enter number of elements in first array
3
Input 3 integers
1
4
6
Input number of elements in second array
3
Input 3 integers
-1
2
3
Sorted array:
-1
1
2
3
4
6
```

Program 13: Program to transpose a matrix.

This C program prints transpose of a matrix. It is obtained by interchanging rows and columns of a matrix. For example if a matrix is

1 2
3 4
5 6

then transpose of above matrix will be,

1 3 5
2 4 6

When we transpose a matrix then the order of matrix changes, but for a square matrix order remains same.

```c
#include <stdio.h>
int main()
{
 int m, n, c, d, matrix[10][10], transpose[10][10];
 printf("Enter the number of rows and columns of matrix ");
 scanf("%d%d",&m,&n);
 printf("Enter the elements of matrix \n");
 for( c = 0 ; c < m ; c++ )
 {
 for( d = 0 ; d < n ; d++ )
 {
 scanf("%d",&matrix[c][d]);
 }
 }
 for( c = 0 ; c < m ; c++ )
 {
 for( d = 0 ; d < n ; d++ )
 {
 transpose[d][c] = matrix[c][d];
 }
 }
 printf("Transpose of entered matrix:-\n");
 for( c = 0 ; c < n ; c++ )
 {
 for( d = 0 ; d < m ; d++ )
 {
 printf("%d\t",transpose[c][d]);
 }
 printf("\n");
 }
 return 0;
}
```

Output:
```
Enter the number of rows and columns of matrix
2
3
Enter the elements of matrix
1  2  3
4  5  6
Transpose of entered matrix
1  4
2  5
3  6
```

Program 14: Program for matrix multiplication.
```c
#include <stdio.h>
int main()
{
  int m, n, p, q, c, d, k, sum = 0;
  int first[10][10], second[10][10], multiply[10][10];
  printf("Enter the number of rows and columns of first matrix\n");
  scanf("%d%d", &m, &n);
  printf("Enter the elements of first matrix\n");
  for ( c = 0 ; c < m ; c++ )
    for ( d = 0 ; d < n ; d++ )
      scanf("%d", &first[c][d]);
  printf("Enter the number of rows and columns of second matrix\n");
  scanf("%d%d", &p, &q);
  if ( n != p )
    printf("Matrices with entered orders can't be multiplied with each other.\n");
  else
  {
    printf("Enter the elements of second matrix\n");
    for ( c = 0 ; c < p ; c++ )
      for ( d = 0 ; d < q ; d++ )
        scanf("%d", &second[c][d]);
    for ( c = 0 ; c < m ; c++ )
    {
      for ( d = 0 ; d < q ; d++ )
```

```c
        {
        for ( k = 0 ; k < p ; k++ )
        {
        sum = sum + first[c][k]*second[k][d];
        }
        multiply[c][d] = sum;
        sum = 0;
        }
        }
        printf("Product of entered matrices:-\n");
        for ( c = 0 ; c < m ; c++ )
        {
        for ( d = 0 ; d < q ; d++ )
        printf("%d\t", multiply[c][d]);
        printf("\n");
        }
        }
    getch();
     return 0;
    }
```

Output:
```
    Enter the number of rows and columns of first matrix
    3
    3
    Enter the elements of first matrix
    1  2  0
    0  0  1
    2  0  1
    Enter the number of rows and columns of second matrix
    3
    3
    Enter the elements of second matrix
    1  1  2
    2  1  1
    1  2  1
    Product of entered matrices:
    5  3  4
    1  2  1
    3  4  5
```

Program 15: Write a program to program to search an element in the array.

```c
#include <stdio.h>
#include<conio.h>
void main()
{
    int a[10], i, item;
    printf("\nEnter elements of an array:\n");
    for (i=0; i<=9; i++)
        scanf("%d", &a[i]);
    printf("\n Enter item to search: ");
    scanf("%d", &item);
    for (i=0; i<=9; i++)
    {
        if (item == a[i])
        {
            printf("\n Item found at location :%d", i+1);
            break;
        }
    }
    if (i > 9)
        printf("\n Item doesnot exist.");
    getch();
}
```

Output
```
Enter elements of an array:
12
34
54
76
23
89
3
77
5
90
Enter item to search : 77
Item found at location : 8
```

5.5 Introduction to String

- A string is an array of characters stored in consecutive memory locations.
- In strings, the ending character is always the null character '\0'. The null character acts as a string terminator.
- **A string is a collection of characters.** Strings are always enlosed in double quotes as "string_constant".
- Strings are used in string handling operations such as,
    - Counting the length of a string.
    - Comparing two strings.
    - Copying one string to another.
    - Converting lower case string to upper case.
    - Converting upper case string to lower case.
    - Joining two strings.
    - Reversing string.

5.5.1 Definition

- Array of character are called strings.

OR

- String is nothing but an array of characters ended with null character ('\0').

OR

- The string is sequence of characters that is treated as a single data item. In general, the character array is called as string.
- A string is an array of characters terminated by a special character called NULL character (i.e. '\0'). Strings are always enclosed in double quotes.

  Example: Suppose that the string "INDIA" is called string and it is stored in memory as:

I	N	D	I	A	\0
2000	2002	2004	2006	2008	2010

- Each character is stored in 1 byte as its ASCII code. Since, the string is stored as an array, it is possible to manipulate individual characters using either subscript or pointer notation.
- Since "INDIA" is a string contains 5 characters. So the array word will be a 6-element array because last character of a string is "\0". The representation can be shown as:

Element No.	Subscript No.	Array Element	Corresponding data item
1	0	word [0]	I
2	1	word [1]	N
3	2	word [2]	D
4	3	word [3]	I
5	4	word [4]	A
6	5	word [5]	\0

5.5.2 Declaration and Initialization

1. **String Declaration:**
   Syntax: `char string_name[length];`
   Example: `char name[4];`
- Also example declares as an array name which can store at the most 4 characters.
- As you know that a string is a character array, then it is declared as follows:
   For example:
   ```
   char name[20];
   char address[20];
   ```
2. **String Initialization:**
- Character arrays can be initialized in two ways - as individual characters or as single string.
   Example:
   ```
   char greet[10] = {'n', 'i', 'r', 'a', 'l', 'i'};
                   // This declaration automatically assigns storage
   char greet[10] = "nirali"
                   // Equivalent to 7 characters including '\0' to
                   the character
   char greet[ ] = "nirali";
                   // Array greet.
   ```
   The compiler automatically stores the null character at the end of the string. The memory representation of char greet[] = "nirali" is given as follows.

| n | i | r | a | l | i | \0 |

Program 5.19: Program to illustrate string as a character array.
```
#include<stdio.h>
void main()
{
   int i;
   char a[] = {'P','R','A','G','A','T','I','\0'};
   char b[] = "PRAGATI";
   clrscr();
   for(i=0;i<7;i++)
    printf("%c", a[i]);
   printf("\n");
   for(i=0;i<7;i++)
    printf("%c", b[i]);
   getch();
}
```
Output:
```
PRAGATI
PRAGATI
```

Program 5.20: Program to accept and display the string.
```
/*accept and display string*/
#include<stdio.h>
#include<conio.h>
void main()
{
char str[20];
clrscr();
printf("Enter name:");
scanf("%s",str);
printf("The entered name is:");
printf("%s",str);
getch();
}
```
Output:
```
Enter name: Rajesh
The entered name is: Rajesh
```

Program 5.21: Program to count the length of the string.
```
#include<stdio.h>
#include<conio.h>
void main()
{
char str[20];
int x=0;
clrscr();
printf("Enter the string: ");
scanf("%s", str);
while(str[x]!='\0')
{
    x++;
}
printf("\nLength of the string is: %d",x);
getch();
}
```
Output:
```
Enter the string: Programming
Length of the string is: 11
```

Program 5.22: Program to count the upper-case characters.

```c
/* count the upper-case characters from the string */
#include<stdio.h>
#include<conio.h>
void main()
{
char str[20];
int x, upper=0;
clrscr();
printf("Enter the string: ");
scanf("%s", str);
for(x=0;str[x]!='\0';x++)
{
if(str[i]>='A' && str[i]<='Z')
upper++;
}
printf("\nUpper case characters are: %d",upper);
getch();
}
```

Output:
```
Enter the string: DnyaNEshWar
Upper case characters are: 4
```

Program 5.23: Program to print reverse of the string.

```c
#include<stdio.h>
#include<conio.h>
void main()
{
   int i=0,j=1;
   char str[50];
   printf("Enter the string: ");
   scanf("%s", str);
   while(str[i]!='\0')
   {
    i++;
   }
   printf("The reverse of the string is:");
   for(j=i;j>=0;j--)
   {
    printf("%c",str[j]);
   }
   getch();
}
```

Output:
```
Enter the string: Rajesh
The reverse of the string is: hsejaR
```

Program 5.24: Program to copy one string to another string.

```c
/* Copy one string to other */
#include<stdio.h>
#include<conio.h>
void main()
{
char str1[10];
char str2[10];
int i=0;
clrscr();
printf("\n Enter the first string: ");
scanf("%s", str1);
printf("\n Enter the second string: ");
scanf("%s", str2);
printf("\n Strings before copying");
printf("\n First string is:%s",str1);
printf("\n Second string is:%s",str2);
for(i=0;i<10;i++)
{
   str2[i]=str1[i];
}
printf("\n Strings After copying");
printf("\n First string is:%s",str1);
printf("\n Second string is:%s",str2);
getch();
}
```

Output:
```
Enter the first string:Rajesh
Enter the second string:Yemul
Strings before copying
First string is: Rajesh
Second string is: Yemul
Strings After copying
First string is: Rajesh
Second string is: Rajesh
```

Program 5.25: Program to compare to strings.
```
#include<stdio.h>
#include<conio.h>
void main()
{
char string1[5],string2[5];
int i,temp = 0;
printf("Enter the string1 value:\n");
scanf("%s",string1);
printf("\nEnter the String2 value:\n");
scanf("%s",string2);
for(i=0; string1[i]!='\0'; i++)
{
   if(string1[i] == string2[i])
     temp = 1;
   else
     temp = 0;
}
if(temp == 1)
printf("Both strings are same.");
else
printf("Both string are not same.");
getch();
}
```

Output 1:
```
Enter the string1 value: Rajesh
Enter the String2 value: Rajendra
Both string are not same.
```

Output 2:
```
Enter the string1 value: Rajesh
Enter the String2 value: Rajesh
Both strings are same.
```

Program 5.26: Program to concatenate two strings.
```
#include<conio.h>
void main()
{
char str1[20];
char str2[20];
int i=0,j=0;
clrscr();
printf("\n Enter the first String :");
scanf("%s",str1);
printf("\n Enter the second String :");
scanf("%s",str2);
while(str1[i]!='\0')
{
    i++;
}
while(str2[j]!='\0')
{
    str1[i]=str2[j];
    i++;
    j++;
}
str1[i]='\0';
printf("\n The concatenated string is : %s",str1)'
getch();
}
```
Output:
```
Enter the first String : Rajesh
the second String : Yemul
The concatenated string is : RajeshYemul
```

Program 5.27: Program to count number of vowels and consonants from the string.
```
#include<stdio.h>
#include<conio.h>
void main()
{
char str[20];
int i=0,cnt1=0,cnt2=0;
clrscr();
printf("\n Enter the String :");
scanf("%s",str);
```

```c
    while(str[i]!='\0')
    {
       if(str[i]=='a' || str[i]=='e' || str[i]=='i' || str[i]=='o' ||
    str[i]=='u' )
       {
        cnt1++;
       }
       else
       {
        cnt2++
       }
       i++;
    }
    printf("\n The entered string is : %s",str);
    printf("\n Vowels=%d and consonants = %d",cnt1.cnt2);
    getch();
    }
```

Output:
```
Enter the String : education
The entered string is : education
Vowels = 5 and consonants = 4
```

Program 5.28: Program to check whether string is palindrome or not.

```c
    #include<stdio.h>
    #include<conio.h>
    void main()
    {
       char str[20];
       int i=0,j=0,flag=0;
       clrscr();
       printf("\n Enter the String :");
       scanf("%s",str);

       while(str[i]!='\0')
       {
        i++;
       }
       i=i-1;
```

```c
        while(j!=i)
        {
         if(str[i]==str[j])
         {
            flag=1;
         }
         else
         {
            flag=2;
            break;
         }
         j++;
         i--;
        }
        if(flag==1)
        {
         printf("%s" is palindrome",str);
        }
        else
        {
         printf("%s" is not palindrome",str);
        }
        getch();
    }
```

Output:

```
    Enter the String : NITIN
    NITIN is palindrome
```

5.6 String Functions

5.6.1 String Character related Functions

- We will see a function which deals with only single characters. These functions are include in the header file, ctype.h'.
- These functions are called as **character related functions**. The various functions are given in the table.

Character Related Function	Purpose
isalnum	Is the character, alphanumeric
isalpha	Is the character, an alphabet
isascii	Is the character, an ASCII character
iscntrl	Is the character, a control character
isdigit	Is the character, a digit
isgraph	Is the character, a graphics character
islower	Is the character, a lower case character
isprint	Is the character, a printable character
ispunct	Is the character, a punctuation character
isspace	Is the character, a space
is upper	Is the character, an upper case character
isxdigit	Is the character, a hexadecimal digit

- All above functions, take a single character, c as an argument. If the condition evaluates to be TRUE, it returns a non-zero value. If the condition evaluates to be FALSE, it returns a zero value.

Program 5.29: Program to illustrate isalpha() function.

```c
#include<stdio.h>
#include<ctype.h>
void main()
{
    char c;
    clrscr();
    puts ("\n Enter a character");
    scanf("%c",&c);
    if (isalpha (c) > 0)
     puts ("The character is an alphabet");
    else
     puts ("The character is not an alphabet");
}
```

Output 1:
```
Enter a character
    v
The character is alphabet
```
Output 2:
```
Enter a character
   2
The character is not alphabet
```

5.6.2 Standard Library Functions

- C library supports various string handling functions which are used to carry the string manipulations. These functions are declared in header file <string.h>.
- Following are some of the most commonly used functions. Consider that string1 and string2 are two string variables.

Function	Purpose
strcpy(string1, string2)	It copies/assigns the content of string2 into string1.
strncpy(string1, string2, n)	It copies only leftmost n characters from string1 into string2.
strcat(string1, string2)	Concatenates (joins) the string2 to end of string1. String2 is appended to string1 by removing null character of string1, placing string2 from there and placing null character at the end.
strncat(string1, string2, n)	Concatenates (joins) the left most n characters of string2 to the end of string1.
strcmp(string1, string2)	Compares two strings Returns = 0 if they are equal >0 if string1 > string2 <0 if string1 < string2 The numeric difference of first non-matching characters of the strings is returned if they are not equal.
stricmp(string1, string2)	Compares two strings, ignoring the case For example: "Nirali" and "nirali" shows equal.
strncmp(string1, string2, n)	Similar to strcmp(), with difference is that, it compares only left most n characters of string1 to string2.
strlen(string1)	Finds the length of specified string i.e. number of characters in the string.
strstr(string1, string2)	It searches whether string2 is contained in string1 If found, returns the position (pointer) of the first occurrence of string2, otherwise it returns NULL pointer.

contd. ...

strchr(string1, ch)	It locates the first occurrence of a character ch into string string1. If found returns pointer, otherwise NULL.
strrchr(string1, ch)	It locates the last occurrence of a character ch into string string1. If found returns pointer, otherwise NULL.
strlwr(string1)	It converts the string1 to lowercase.
strupr(string1)	It converts the string1 to uppercase.
atoi(string1)	Converts string1 into an integer, returning the result. Similarly there is atol() and atof().
strset(string1,ch)	It sets character ch to all positions of string string1.

- C also supports various library functions, which are dealing with single characters.

Program 5.30: Program to accept a string. Convert it to uppercase, if first character is capital letter. Otherwise convert it to lowercase.

```
#include<string.h>
#include<ctype.h>
void main()
{
    char str[20];
    clrscr();
    printf("Enter a string:");
    gets(str);
    if (isupper(str[0])) //or (str[0]>='A' && str[0]<='Z')
    strupr(str);
    else
    strlwr(str);
    printf("Converted string: %s",str);
    getch();
}
```

Output:
```
Enter a string:Nirali Prakashan
Converted string: NIRALI PRAKASHAN
Enter a string:nirali Prakashan
Converted string: nirali prakashan
```

1. strlen( ) Function:
- This string function gives the length of a string.
  Syntax: strlen(s1)

Program 5.31: Program for strlen() function.
```
#include <stdio.h>
#include <string.h>
int main()
{
 char a[100];
 int length;
 printf("Enter a string to calculate it's length\n");
 gets(a);
 length = strlen(a);
 printf("Length of entered string is = %d\n",length);
 getch():
 return 0;
}
```
Output:
```
Enter a string to calculate it's length
Programming simplified
Length of entered string is = 22
```

2. strcpy( ) Function:
- This string function used for copying one string to another string.
  Syntax: strcpy (string1, string2)

Program 5.32: Program for strcat() and strcpy() functions.
```
#include<stdio.h>
#include<string.h>
void main( )
{
    char s1[45] ;
    char blank[] = " ", c[] = "Practice !", prog[] = "Programming";
    char good[] = "Good";
    strcpy(s1,good);
    strcat(s1,blank);
    strcat(s1, prog);
    strcat(s1, blank);
    strcat(s1, c);
    puts(s1);
    getch();
}
```
Output:
```
Good Programming Practice!
```

3. strcat( ) Function:

- This string function concatenates (combine/joins) two or more strings. For joining or combining two string strcat( ) is used.

   Syntax: strcat (string1, string2)

Program 5.33: Program to concatenate two strings using strcat( ) function.

```
#include <stdio.h>
#include <string.h>
int main()
{
 char a[100], b[100];
 printf("Enter the first string\n");
 gets(a);
 printf("Enter the second string\n");
 gets(b);
 strcat(a,b);
 printf("String obtained on concatenation is %s\n",a);
 getch();
 return 0;
}
```

Output:
```
Enter the first string
Programming
Enter the second string
Simplified
String obtained on concatenation is Programming Simplified
```

4. strcmp( ) Function:

- This string function used for comparing two strings:

   Syntax: strcmp (string1, string2)

Program 5.34: Program for strcmp() function.

```
#include <stdio.h>
#include <string.h>
int main()
{
 char a[100], b[100];
 printf("Enter the first string\n");
 gets(a);
```

```
    printf("Enter the second string\n");
    gets(b);
    if( strcmp(a,b) == 0 )
    printf("Entered strings are equal.\n");
    else
    printf("Entered strings are not equal.\n");
    getch();
    return 0;
}
```

Output:
```
Enter the first string
simplified the program
Enter the second string
Simplified
Entered strings are not equal.
```

Program 5.35: Program to swap two strings.
```
#include <stdio.h>
#include <string.h>
#include <malloc.h>
int main()
{
 char first[100], second[100], *temp;
 printf("Enter the first string\n");
 gets(first);
 printf("Enter the second string\n");
 gets(second);
 printf("\nBefore Swapping\n");
 printf("First string: %s\n",first);
 printf("Second string: %s\n\n",second);
 temp = (char*)malloc(100);
 strcpy(temp,first);
 strcpy(first,second);
 strcpy(second,temp);
 printf("After Swapping\n");
 printf("First string: %s\n",first);
 printf("Second string: %s\n",second);
 getch();
 return 0;
}
```

Output:
```
Enter the first string
hello
Enter the second string
bye
Before Swapping
First string: hello
Second string: bye
After Swapping
First string: bye
Second string: hello
```

5.7 Implementation without Standard Library Functions

- Following programs describes implementation of string without using standard library functions.

Program 5.36: Program to concat two strings without using library function.
```
#include<stdio.h>
#include<string.h>
void concat(char[],char[]);
void main()
{
char s1[50],s2[30];
printf("\nEnter String 1:");
gets(s1);
printf("\nEnter String 2:");
gets(s2);
concat(s1,s2);
printf("\nConcated string is:%s",s1);
getch();
}
void concat(char s1[],char s2[])
{
int i,j;
i = strlen(s1);
for(j=0; s2[j] != ' '; i++,j++)
s1[i]=s2[j];
s1[i]=' ';
}
```
Output:
```
Enter String 1: Amar
Enter String 2: Salunkhe
Concated string is: AmarSalunkhe
```

Program 5.37: Reverse string without using library function.
```
#include<stdio.h>
#include<string.h>
void main()
{
 char str[100],temp;
 int i,j=0;
 printf("\nEnter the string:");
 gets(str);
 i=0;
 j=strlen(str)-1;
 while(i<j)
 {
 temp=str[i];
 str[i]=str[j];
 str[j]=temp;
 i++;
 j--;
 }
 printf("\nReverse string is:%s",str);
 getch();
}
```
Output:
```
Enter the string: Amar
Reverse string is: ramA
```

Program 5.38: Program for comparison of two strings.
```
#include<stdio.h>
#include<conio.h>
void main()
{
char str1[30],str2[30];
int i;
printf("\n Enter two strings:");
gets(str1);
gets(str2);
```

```
    //loop for comparison
    i=0;
    while(str1[i]==str2[i] && str1[i]!=' ')
    i++;
    if(str1[i] > str2[i])
    printf("\nstr1 > str2");
    else
    if(str1[i] < str2[i])
    printf("\nstr1 < str2");
    else
    printf("\nstr1 = str2");
    getch();
    }
```
Output:
```
    Enter two strings!
    Vijay
    Amar
    str1 > str2
```

Program 5.39: Program to copy one string into other without using library function.
```
    #include<stdio.h>
    #include<conio.h>
    void main()
    {
    char s1[100],s2[100];
    int i;
    //reading a string and finding its length
    printf("nEnter the string:");
    gets(s1);
    i=0;
    while(s1[i]!=' ')
    {
    s2[i]=s1[i];
    i++;
    }
    //since the ' ' is not copied
    s2[i]='';
    printf("\nCopied String is %s ",s2);
    getch();
    }
```
Output:
```
    Enter the string: AmarSalunkhe
    Copied String is AmarSalunkhe
```

Program 5.40: Program to find length of string without using library function.
```c
#include<stdio.h>
#include<conio.h>
void main()
{
 char str[100];
 int length;
 printf("\nEnter the String: ");
 gets(str);
 length = 0; // Initial Length
 while(str[length]!='\0')
 length++;
 printf("\nLength of the String is: %d",length);
 getch();
}
```
Output:
```
Enter the String: Amar
Length of String is: 4
```

Programs on String

Program 1: Program to copy contents of one array into another array.
```c
/* Program to copy contents of one array into another array */
#include<stdio.h>
#include<conio.h>
void main()
{
    float a1[50], a2[50];
    int i, n;
    printf("Input the no. of elements to be used of the array \n");
    scanf("%d",&n);
    for(i=0;i<n;i++)
    {
     printf("Input the %d element of the array:", i+1);
     scanf("%d", &a1[i]);
    }
    for(i=0;i<n;i++)
     a2[i]=a1[i];
    printf("Print the 2nd array\n");
    for (i=0;i<n;i++)
     printf("%d\t",a2[i]);
    getch();
}
```

Output:

```
Input the no. of elements to be used of the array 3
Input the 1 element of array: 1
Input the 2 element of array: 2
Input the 3 element of array: 3
Print the 2nd array 1  2  3
```

Program 2: Program to find the number of vowels, consonants, digits and white space in a program.

```c
#include<stdio.h>
int main(){
char line[150];
int i,v,c,ch,d,s,o;
o=v=c=ch=d=s=0;
printf("Enter a line of string:\n");
gets(line);
for(i=0;line[i]!='\0';++i)
{
if(line[i]=='a' || line[i]=='e' || line[i]=='i' || line[i]=='o' ||
line[i]=='u' || line[i]=='A' || line[i]=='E' || line[i]=='I' || line
[i]=='O' ||line[i]=='U')
++v;
else if((line[i]>='a'&& line[i]<='z') || (line[i]>='A'&& line[i]<='Z'))
++c;
else if(line[i]>='0'&&c<='9')
++d;
else if (line[i]==' ')
++s;
}
printf("Vowels: %d",v);
printf("\nConsonants: %d",c);
printf("\nDigits: %d",d);
printf("\nWhite spaces: %d",s);
getch();
return 0;
}
```

Output:
```
Enter a line of string;
This program is easy 2 understand
Vowels: 9
Consonants: 18
Digits: 1
White spaces: 5
```

Program 3: Program to convert string to integer.
```
#include<stdio.h>
#include<stdlib.h>
void main()
{
int num;
// Variable marks is of Char Type
char marks[3] = "98";
printf("Please Enter Marks: ");
scanf("%s",marks);
num = atoi(marks);
printf("\nMarks: %d",num);
getch();
}
```

Output:
```
Please Enter Marks: 76
Marks: 76
```

Program 4: Convert given string into uppercase using library function.
```
#include<stdio.h>
#include<conio.h>
#include<string.h>
void main()
{
char *string = "Amar Salunkhe";
printf("String before to strupr: %s\n", string);
strupr(string);
printf("String after strupr: %s\n", string);
getch();
}
```

Output:
```
String before to strupr: Amar Salunkhe
String after strupr: AMAR SALUNKHE
```

Program 5: Program count total number of capital and small letters from accepted.
```
#include<stdio.h>
#include<conio.h>
void main()
{
int upper=0,lower=0;
char ch[80];
int i;
clrscr();
printf("nEnter The String: ");
gets(ch);
i=0;
while(ch[i]!='\0')
 {
 if(ch[i]>='A' && ch[i]<='Z')
 upper++;
 if(ch[i]>='a' && ch[i]<='z')
 lower++;
 i++;
 }
 printf("nUppercase Letters: %d",upper);
 printf("nLowercase Letters: %d",lower);
 getch();
 }
```
Output:
```
Enter The String: Amar U Salunkhe
Uppercase Letters: 3
Lowercase Letters: 10
```

Program 6: Program to convert given string into lowercase using library function.
```
#include<stdio.h>
#include<conio.h>
#include<string.h>
void main()
{
char *string = "Amar Salunkhe";
printf("\nString before to strlwr: %sn", string);
strlwr(string);
printf("\nString after strlwr: %sn", string);
getch();
}
```
Output:
```
String before to strlwr: Amar Salunkhe
String after strlwr: amar salunkhe
```

Questions

1. What is meant by array and string? Explain with the help of example.
2. How to declare an array? How to access an individual array element?
3. What is meant by dimensions of an array? Explain two-dimensional array with suitable example. How do you declare two-dimensional array?
4. Why nested loops are required in some applications of multidimensional arrays?
5. Write a program that uses an array to store a maximum of 20 test scores and calculate their average.
6. Write a program which will read 15 positive integer and then
   (a) Find all pairs of elements whose sum is 20.
   (b) Determine the number of odd and even numbers.
7. Given two one dimensional arrays A and B which are sorted in ascending order. Write a program to merge them into a single sorted array C that contains every item from array A and B in ascending order.
8. Write a program which will read a string and rewrite it in the alphabetical order. e.g. DRAWING should be written as ADGINRW.
9. Write a program to replace a particular word by another word in a given string. e.g. the word bright should be replaced by pleasant in the text.
   "Today, it is a bright day"
10. Explain the term character array with example.
11. Explain different character and string manipulation functions.
12. Define string?
13. What are the advantages and disadvantages of using arrays.
14. Write a program to print pascal triangle using array.
15. Is "C" a string or a character?
16. What is the difference between integer array and character array?
17. Write a small program to convert string entered by user to uppercase characters and display the string.
18. What will be the output of following:

    (a) ```
        main( )
        {
            char name[] = {'S', 'E', 'E', 'D'};
            printf("\n %s",name);
        }
        ```
        ```

(b) ```
    main( )
    {
        char *p = "alqc";
        printf("%c ...", +++ (p++));
        printf("%c", * ++p);
    }
```

19. With suitable example following string functions.
    (a) strlen( )
    (b) strcmp( )
    (c) strcat( )
    (d) strcpy( )
```

Chapter 6...

Structures and Union

Contents ...

6.1 Introduction to Structure
    6.1.1 Definition
    6.1.2 Declaration and Initializing Structure
    6.1.3 Accessing Members of Structure
6.2 Operations on Structures
6.3 Nested Structure
6.4 Introduction to Union
    6.4.1 Definition
    6.4.2 Declaration and Initialization
    6.4.3 Accessing Members of Union
6.5 Difference between Structure and Union
- Questions

6.1 Introduction to Structure

- Structure is analogous to records. A structure is a user defined data type. A structure is a convenient tool for handling a group of logically related data items.
- Structure is a collection of logically related data items of different data types grouped together under a single name.

6.1.1 Definition

- Structure is user defined data type which is used to store heterogeneous data under unique name.

OR

- Structure is a collection of different data types which are grouped together and each element in a structure is called member.
- To define a structure, you must use the struct statement. The struct statement defines a new data type, with more than one member for your program. The format of the struct statement is this:

```
struct [structure tag]
{
 member definition;
 member definition;
 ...
 member definition;
} [one or more structure variables];
```

- The structure tag is optional and each member definition is a normal variable definition, such as int i; or float f; or any other valid variable definition. At the end of the structure's definition, before the final semicolon, you can specify one or more structure variables but it is optional. Here is the way you would declare the Book structure:

```
struct Books
{
 char title[50];
 char author[50];
 char subject[100];
 int book_id;
} book;
```

6.1.2 Declaration and Initializing Structure

1. **Declaration of Structure:**
- To define or declare a structure you can use struct keyword.

   Syntax:
   ```
   struct structure_name
   {
    <data-type> element 1;
    <data-type> element 2;
        :
    :
    <data-type> element n;
   }struct_var;
   ```

   Example:
   ```
   struct emp_info
   {
    char emp_id[10];
    char name[100];
    float sal;
   }emp;
   ```

Note:
- Structure is always terminated with semicolon (;).
- Structure name as emp_info can be later used to declare structure variables of its type in a program.

2. **Initializing Structure:**
- C programming language treats a structure as a custom data type therefore you can initialize a structure like a variable.

- Here, is an example of initialize product structure:
    ```
    struct product
    {
      char name[50];
      double price;
    } book = {"C programming language" 40.5 "};
    ```
- In above example, we define product structure, then we declare and initialize.

How to Declare Structure Variables?:
- We are already seen how to declare structure. But we cannot use it in the program, since it is not a variable name. Hence, we cannot assign any values, cannot perform arithmetic and logical operations.
- To perform all such actions, we need to associate structure variable with the structure type.
- There are three methods of associating structure variables with the structure-type.
    (a) Structure-variable names in structure declaration.
    (b) Structure-variables as data declarations.
    (c) Array of structure-variables.

1. **Structure-variable Names in Structure Declaration:**
- The structure declaration may contain structure variable names for structure-variables.

    Syntax:
    ```
    struct structure-name
    {
    data-type1    element 1;
    data-type2    element 2;
    :
    :
    data-type n   element n;
    } var 1, var 2, …… var n;
    ```

    For example:
    ```
    struct employee
    {
        char empname[20];
        char empcode[6];
        float basic;
    }  emp1, emp2, emp3;
    ```
    Here, emp 1, emp 2, emp 3 are three variables of structure type employee.

2. **Structure-variables as Data Declarations:**
- A structure variables declaration can be made as data type declaration since structure-type is a programmer derived data type.

    For example:
    ```
    struct employee
    {
        char empname[20];
        char empcode[6];
        float basic;
    };
    main ()
    static struct emp1, emp2, emp3;
    ```
    where, emp1, emp2, emp3 are three variables of structure type-employee.

3. **Array of Structure Variables:**
- If we try to use the methods above for declaring 100 employee's details, we will require 100 structure variable names which is not possible.
- The solution is that to declare arrays. Structure variable declaration can be made as array of structure-variable declaration.

    For example:
    ```
    struct employee
    {
        char empname[20];
        char empcode[6];
        float basic;
    };
    struct employee emp[100];
    ```

6.1.3 Accessing Members of Structures
- The variables which are declared inside the structure are called as members of structure.
- Structure members can be accessed using member operator '.' . It is also called as 'dot operator' or 'period operator'.

    Syntax:
    ```
    structure_var.member;
    ```

Program 6.1: Program to demonstrate structure.
```
#include<stdio.h>
#include<conio.h>
struct comp_info
{
    char nm[100];
    char addr[100];
}info;
```

```c
void main()
{
   clrscr();
   printf("\n Enter Company Name: ");
   gets(info.nm);
   printf("\n Enter Address: ");
   gets(info.addr);
   printf("\n\n Company Name: %s",info.nm);
   printf("\n\n Address: %s",info.addr);
   getch();
}
```
Output:
```
Enter Company Name: Nirali Prakashan
Enter Address: Pune, Maharashtra, INDIA
Company Name: Nirali Prakashan
Address: Pune, Maharashtra, INDIA
```

Program 6.2: Program for structure.
```c
#include <stdio.h>
#include <string.h>
struct Books
{
 char title[50];
 char author[50];
 char subject[100];
 int book_id;
};
int main( )
{
 struct Books Book1; /* Declare Book1 of type Book */
 struct Books Book2; /* Declare Book2 of type Book */
 /* book 1 specification */
 strcpy( Book1.title, "C Programming");
 strcpy( Book1.author, "Rajesh Yemul");
 strcpy( Book1.subject, "C Programming Tutorial");
 Book1.book_id = 1121;
 /* book 2 specification */
```

```c
    strcpy( Book2.title, "Basic of C++");
    strcpy( Book2.author, "B. Chaudhary");
    strcpy( Book2.subject, "Basics of C++ Tutorial");
    Book2.book_id = 2172;
    /* print Book1 info */
    printf( "Book 1 title: %s\n", Book1.title);
    printf( "Book 1 author: %s\n", Book1.author);
    printf( "Book 1 subject: %s\n", Book1.subject);
    printf( "Book 1 book_id: %d\n", Book1.book_id);
    /* print Book2 info */
    printf( "Book 2 title: %s\n", Book2.title);
    printf( "Book 2 author: %s\n", Book2.author);
    printf( "Book 2 subject: %s\n", Book2.subject);
    printf( "Book 2 book_id: %d\n", Book2.book_id);
    getch();
    return 0;
}
```

Output:

```
Book 1 title: C Programming
Book 1 author: Rajesh Yemul
Book 1 subject: C Programming Tutorial
Book 1 book_id: 1121
Book 2 title: Basic of C++
Book 2 author: B.Chaudhary
Book 2 subject: Basics of C++ Tutorial
Book 2 book_id: 2172
```

Program 6.3: Program to demonstrate the initialization of structures.

```c
#include<stdio.h>
#include<conio.h>
void main()
{
    struct student
    {
      int roll_no;
      char name[25];
      float per;
    };
```

```c
    struct student s={10,"Rajesh",84.27};
    printf("\n Roll No=%d",s.roll_no);
    printf("\n Name =%s",s.name);
    printf("\n Percentage =%f",s.per);
    getch();
}
```

Output:
```
Roll No = 10
Name = Rajesh
Percentage = 84.269997
```

Program 6.4: Program to accept structure members from the user and display them.
```c
#include<stdio.h>
void main()
{
    struct book
    {
        int book_id;
        char book_name[10];
        float  price;
    }s;
    printf("\n Enter book-id, name and price: \n");
    scanf("%d%s%d", &s.book-id, s.book_name, &s.price);
    printf("\n Entered information: ");
    printf("\n Book_ID: %d", s.book_id);
    printf("\n Book_Name: %s", s.book_name);
    printf("\n Price: %d",s.price);
    getch();
}
```

Output:
```
Enter book-id, name and price:
1265   C 225
Entered information:
Book_ID: 1265
Book_Name: C
Price: 225
```

Program 6.5: Program to Declare a structure 'struct_time' having data members hour, minutes, seconds. Accept this data and display the time in format 18:25:30.

```
#include<stdio.h>
#include<conio.h>
struct struct_time
{
   int hour;
   int minutes;
   int seconds;
}T;
void main()
{
clrscr();
printf("\n Enter Hours : ");
scanf("%d",&.hour);
printf("\n Enter Minutes : ");
scanf("%d",&T.minutes);
printf("\n Enter Seconds : ");
scanf("%d",&T.seconds);
printf("\n Time is : %d:%d:%d",T.hour,T.minutes,T.seconds);
getch();
}
```

Output:
```
Enter Hours : 11
Enter Minutes : 32
Enter Seconds : 45
Time is : 11:32:45
```

Program 6.6: Program to Declare a structure describing 'circle' having data members as radius, perimeter and area. Accept radius and display area and perimeter.

```
#include<stdio.h>
#include<conio.h>
struct circle
{
int radius;
float peri;
float area;
}a;
```

```
void main()
{
clrscr();
printf("\n Enter radius : ");
scanf("%d",&a.radius);
a.peri = 2.0 * 3.14 * (float) a.radius;
printf("\n Perimeter : %.2f",a.peri);
a.area = 3.14 * (float)(a.radius * a.radius);
printf("\n Area: %.2f",a.area);
getch();
}
```

Output:

```
Enter radius : 12
Perimeter : 75.36
Area: 452.16
```

Array of Structures:

- Structure are often arrayed.
- To declare an array of structures, you must first define a structure and then declare an array variable of that type.
- General **syntax** of array,

    `data-type array-name [size of array];`

    For example:

    `struct emp elist [50];`

- Taking the example of employees, here we declare array of structure. We access array elements using index of array i.e. num[0], num[1] ...... etc. But here elements of array are structures and each number of structure is accessed by '.' operator. Hence, member can be obtained using,

    `array-name [index].member-name`

- Hence, to access basic of 3rd employee, we say elist[2].basic (if starting index is '0'). elist[2] gives the entire structure for 3rd employee & elist[2] basic gives salary for 3rd employee.

Program 6.7: Program to calculate net pay of 50 employees.

```c
/* A program to calculate net pay */
#include<stdio.h>
void main()
{
struct emp
{
 char ename[20];
 char ecode[6];
 float basic;
 float hra, da;
 float npay;
} e[50];
int i;
for(i=0;i<49;i++)
{
printf("\n Enter name of employee:");
scanf("%s", &e[i].ename);
printf("\n Enter ecode of employee:");
scanf("%s", &e[i].ecode);
printf("\n Enter basic pay:");
scanf("%f", &e[i].basic);
printf("\n Enter HRA:");
scanf("%f", &e[i].hra);
printf("\n Enter DA:");
scanf("%f", &e[i].da);
}
for(i=0;i<49;i++)
{
e[i].npay = e[i].basic + e[i].hra + e[i].da;
printf("\n Name Ecode Basic pay HRA DA Net pay");
printf("\n %s %s %f %f %f %f",
e[i].ename, e[i].ecode, e[i].basic, e[i].hra, e[i].da, e[i].netpay);
}
}
```

Program 6.8: Write a program to use structure within union, display the contents of structure elements.

```c
#include<stdio.h>
#include<conio.h>
void main()
{
 struct student
 {
 char name[30];
 char sex;
 int rollno;
 float percentage;
 };
 union details
 {
 struct student st;
 };
 union details set;
 clrscr();
 printf("Enter details:");
 printf("\nEnter name: ");
 scanf("%s", set.st.name);
 printf("\nEnter rollno: ");
 scanf("%d", &set.st.rollno);
 flushall();
 printf("\nEnter sex: ");
 scanf("%c",&set.st.sex);
 printf("\nEnter percentage: ");
 scanf("%f",&set.st.percentage);
 printf("\nThe student details are:n");
 printf("Name: %s", set.st.name);
 printf("\nRollno: %d", set.st.rollno);
 printf("\nSex: %c", set.st.sex);
 printf("\nPercentage: %f", set.st.percentage);
 getch();
}
```

Output:

```
Enter details:
Enter name: Amar
Enter rollno: 10
Enter sex: M
Enter percentage: 89
The student details are:
Name: Amar
Rollno: 10
Sex: M
Percentage: 89.0000
```

6.2 Operations on Structures

- There is a relatively small number of operations which C directly supports on structures. As we have seen, we can define structures, declare variables of structure type and select the members of structures.
- We can also assign entire structures: the expression,
    ```
    c1 = c2
    ```
    would assign all of c2 to c1 (both the real and imaginary parts, assuming the preceding declarations). We can also pass structures as arguments to functions and declare and define functions which return structures. But to do anything else, we typically have to write our own code (often as functions). For example, we could write a function to add two complex numbers:
    ```
    struct complex
    cpx_add(struct complex c1, struct complex c2)
    {
      struct complex sum;
      sum.real = c1.real + c2.real;
      sum.imag = c1.imag + c2.imag;
      return sum;
    }
    ```
    We could then say things like,
    ```
    c1 = cpx_add(c2, c3)
    ```
- One more thing you can do with a structure is initialize a structure variable declaring it. As for array initializations, the initializer consists of a comma-separated list of values enclosed in brances { }:
    ```
    struct complex c1 = {1, 2};
    struct complex c2 = {3, 4};
    ```
- Of course, the type of each initializer in the list must be compatible with the type of the corresponding structure member.

6.3 Nested Structure

- C language allows a member of a structure can be a structure itself. Such structure declarations with some members as themselves being structures is called as **nested/embedded structure**.
- The nested structure must be declared before it is declared as a member of another structure.
- When a member of a structure has to be further broken down into entities, that member can be declared as structure.
- Nested structure are used in such events, where multiple data items related to each other, are repeated within a structure.

Syntax:
```
struct structure_name
{
   <data-type> element 1;
   <data-type> element 2;
   - - - - - - - - - -
   - - - - - - - - - -
   <data-type> element n;
struct structure_name
   {
      <data-type> element 1;
      <data-type> element 2;
      - - - - - - - - - -
      - - - - - - - - - -
      <data-type> element n;
   } inner_struct_var;
} outer_struct_var;
```

Program 6.9: Program to demonstrate nested structures.
```
#include<stdio.h>
#include<conio.h>
struct stud_Res
{
   int rno;
   char std[10];
   struct stud_Marks
   {
      char subj_nm[30];
      int subj_mark;
   }marks;
}result;
```

```c
void main()
{
    clrscr();
    printf("\n\t Enter Roll Number: ");
    scanf("%d",&result.rno);
    printf("\n\t Enter Standard: ");
    scanf("%s",result.std);
    printf("\n\t Enter Subject Code: ");
    scanf("%s",result.marks.subj_nm);
    printf("\n\t Enter Marks: ");
    scanf("%d",&result.marks.subj_mark);
    printf("\n\n\t Roll Number: %d",result.rno);
    printf("\n\n\t Standard: %s",result.std);
    printf("\n\n\tSubject Code: %s",result.marks.subj_nm);
    printf("\n\n\t Marks: %d",result.marks.subj_mark);
    getch();
}
```

Output:

```
Enter Roll Number: 1
Enter Standard: BCAII
Enter Subject Code: SUB001
Enter Marks: 63
Roll Number: 1
Standard: BCAII
Subject Code: SUB001
Marks: 63
```

Program 6.10: Write a C program to add two distances entered by user. Measurement of distance should be in inch and feet.(Note: 12 inches = 1 foot).

```c
#include <stdio.h>
struct Distance
{
int feet;
float inch;
}d1,d2,sum;
```

```
int main()
{
printf("1st distance\n");
printf("Enter feet: ");
scanf("%d",&d1.feet); /* input of feet for structure variable d1 */
printf("Enter inch: ");
scanf("%f",&d1.inch); /* input of inch for structure variable d1 */
printf("2nd distance\n");
printf("Enter feet: ");
scanf("%d",&d2.feet); /* input of feet for structure variable d2 */
printf("Enter inch: ");
scanf("%f",&d2.inch); /* input of inch for structure variable d2 */
sum.feet=d1.feet+d2.feet;
sum.inch=d1.inch+d2.inch;
if (sum.inch>12){ //If inch is greater than 12, changing it to feet.
++sum.feet;
sum.inch=sum.inch-12;
}
printf("Sum of distances=%d\'-%.1f\"",sum.feet,sum.inch);
/* printing sum of distance d1 and d2 */
return 0;
getch();
}
```

Output:
```
1st distance
Enter feet: 12
Enter inch: 7.9
2nd distance
Enter feet: 2
Enter inch: 9.8
Sum of distance = 15' – 5.1"
```

6.4 Introduction to Union

- A union is a memory location that is shard by more than two different types of variables.
- Union is user defined data type used to stored data under unique variable name at single memory location.
- Union is similar to that of structure. Syntax of union is similar to structure. But the major difference between structure and union is 'storage.'

- In structures, each member has its own storage location, whereas all the members of union use the same, location. Union contains many members of different types, it can handle only one member at a time.

6.4.1 Definition
- A union is a special data type available in C that enables you to store different data types in the same memory location.

OR

- Union is a data type with two or more member similar to structure but in this case all the members share a common memory location. The size of the union corresponds to the length of the largest member. Since the member share a common location they have the same starting address.
- To define a union, you must use the union statement in very similar was as you did while defining structure. The union statement defines a new data type, with more than one member for your program. The format of the union statement is as follows:

```
union [union tag]
{
 member definition;
 member definition;
 ...
 member definition;
} [one or more union variables];
```

- The union tag is optional and each member definition is a normal variable definition, such as int i; or float f; or any other valid variable definition. At the end of the union's definition, before the final semicolon, you can specify one or more union variables but it is optional. Here is the way you would define a union type named Data which has the three members i, f, and str:

```
union Data
{
 int i;
 float f;
 char str[20];
} data;
```

6.4.2 Declaration and Initialization
- To declare union data type, 'union' keyword is used.
- Union holds value for one data type which requires larger storage among their members.

Syntax:

```
union union_name
{
   <data-type> element 1;
   <data-type> element 2;
   <data-type> element 3;
} union_variable;
```

Example:
```
union NiraliPrakashan
{
int comp_id;
char nm;
float sal;
}NP;
```
- In above example, it declares NP variable of type union. The union contains three members as data type of int, char, float. We can use only one of them at a time.

Memory Allocation:

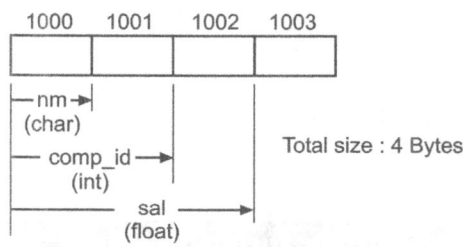

Fig 6.1: Memory allocation for union

- To access union members, we can use the following syntax.
    NP.comp_id
    NP.nm
    NP.sal

6.4.3 Accessing Members of Union
- The member of union are accessed in the same way as structure members are accessed using the '.' operator or → operator.

Syntax:
    union_name.member
            OR
    union_name→member

For example:
```
union id {
    char color[12];
    int size;
    }    shirt;
```

Program 6.11: Program to demonstrate union.
```
#include<stdio.h>
#include<conio.h>
union Pragati
{
   int id;
   char nm[50];
}NP;
```

```
void main()
{
   clrscr();
   printf("\n\t Enter developer id: ");
   scanf("%d", &NP.id);
   printf("\n\n\t Enter developer name: ");
   scanf("%s", NP.nm);
   printf("\n\n Developer ID: %d", NP.id);//Garbage
   printf("\n\n Developed By: %s", NP.nm);
   getch();
}
```
Output:
```
   Enter developer id: 101
   Enter developer name: Nirali
   Developer ID: 26990
   Developed By: Nirali
```

6.5 Difference between Structure and Union

Union	Structure
1. Union allocates one common storage space for all its members.	1. Structure allocates storage space for all its members separately.
2. In Union only one member can be active at a time.	2. In Structure all members can be active at a time.
3. All members in the Union share the same storage area in the computer's memory.	3. Each member in the Structure is assigned its own unique storage area.
4. Conservation of memory.	4. Occupies lot of memory space.
5. Union allocates the memory equal to the maximum memory required by the member.	5. Structure allocates the memory equal to total memory required by all the members.
6. In Union only the first member of a union variable can be initialized.	6. In Structure all members of a structure variable can be initialized.
7. We can access only one member of union at a time.	7. We can access all members of structure at a time.

8. The syntax of union declaration is
union union_name
{
type element 1;
type element 2;
…………..
type element n;
};
	8. The syntax of structure declaration is
	struct structure_name
	{
	type element 1;
	type element 2;
	…………..
	type element n;
	};

contd. ...

9. Example:	9. Example:
| ```
union student
{
int mark;
char name[6];
double average;
};
``` | ```
struct student
{
int mark;
char name[6];
double average;
};
``` |

Programs

Program 1: Program for calculating area of the circle using structure.
```
#include<stdio.h>
#include<conio.h>
void main()
{
    struct circle
    {
        float area;
        float radius;
    };
    struct circle one;
    printf("\n Enter radius:");
    scanf("%f",&one.radius);
    one.area=3.1415*one.radius*one.radius;
    printf("\n area = %f ",one.area);
    getch();
}
```
Output:
```
Enter radius: 12
area = 452.376007
```

Program 2: A sample program to illustrate the use of unions.
```
#include<stdio.h>
int main()
{
union data
{
char a;
int x;
float f;
} myData;
int mode = 1;
myData.a = 'A';
```

```
printf("Here is the Data:\n%c\n%i\n%.3f\n",
                                myData.a, myData.x, myData.f );
myData.x = 42;
mode = 2;
printf("Here is the Data:\n%c\n%i\n%.3f\n",
                                myData.a, myData.x, myData.f );
myData.f = 101.357;
mode = 3;
printf("Here is the Data:\n%c\n%i\n%.3f\n",
                                myData.a, myData.x, myData.f );
if( mode == 1 )
printf("The char is being used\n");
else if( mode == 2 )
printf("The int is being used\n");
else if( mode == 3 )
printf("The float is being used\n");
getch();
return 0;
}
```

Questions

1. What is meant by structure?
2. What is an union?
3. With suitable example explain the nested structure.
4. What is the use of a structure? Explain with example.
5. Difference between structure and union.
6. How to declare and initialise structure? Give an example.
7. Can a function return a value of type 'pointer to structure'?
8. Write a program to read roll numbers and names and total marks of 10 students. Display the data alphabetically sort on name.
9. A structure stores the details of 15 books. Details include the title, price, number of pages, publication and popularity in grades.
   Grade   'A' for highest popularity
           'B' for average
           'C' for low popularity.
   Write a program to print details of the books which has highest popularity.
10. Explain declaration of union and accessing members of union.
11. Write a simple program for unions.
12. How to accessing members of structure?
13. Enlist various operations on structure.
14. Write short note on: Accessing Members of Union.

■■■

Chapter 7...

C Preprocessor

Contents ...

7.1 Introduction
7.2 Definition of Preprocessor
7.3 Macro Substitution Directives
7.4 File Inclusion Directives
7.5 Conditional Compilation Directives
- Questions

7.1 Introduction

- Preprocessor is a macro processor program that processes the code before it passes through the compiler. It operates under the control of preprocessor command lines and directives.
- Preprocessor directives are placed in the source program before the main line before the source code passes through the compiler it is examined by the preprocessor for any preprocessor directives. If there is any appropriate actions are taken then the source program is handed over to the compiler.
- It is called a macro processor because it allows you to define macros, which are brief abbreviations for longer constructs.
- Preprocessor directives follow the special syntax rules and begin with the symbol #.

7.2 Definition of Preprocessor

- A preprocessor is a program that processes our program before it is passed to the compiler for compilation.

OR

- Preprocessor directives are actually the instructions to the compiler itself. They are not translated but are operated directly by the compiler.
- The commands of a preprocessor are called preprocessor directives. Each preprocessor directive begins with a # symbol.
- These statements are called as **'directives'** because they give direction to the preprocessor to take a certain action after reading these directives.
- The block diagram of preprocessor is shown in Fig. 7.1.

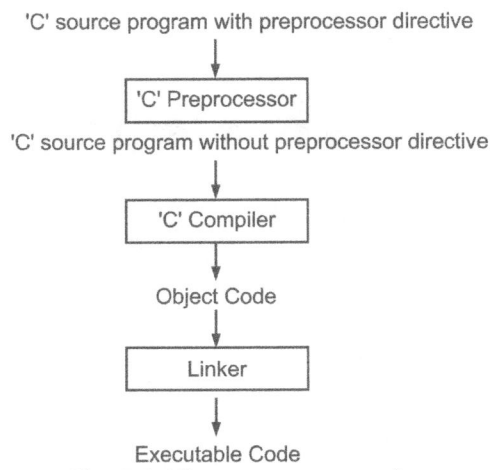

Fig. 7.1: 'C' program processing

- From 'C' source program, the preprocessor removes all the directives i.e. the statements that start with '#' after taking actions. This source code without directives is passed on to 'C' compiler.
- The compiler converts 'C' source program which is without preprocessor directive to the object code. The linker links the object code with the standard library files to get the executable code.
- Preprocessor directives can be placed anywhere in the 'C' program. But, they are generally placed at the beginning of the program before main(). They can be recognised as 'C' program statements starting with '#'.

Note: Preprocessor directives are not terminated with a semicolon (;).

7.3 Macro Substitution Directives

- A micro is a small subprogram which contains executable code.
- A micro is similar to a function.
- An argumented macro is also called a function macro and the macroname can have arguments.
- A macro can be nested within another macro this is called as nesting of macros.
- Micro substitution directive replaces every occurrence of a simple macro in the program.
- Micro substitution is obtained using #*define directive*.
- **#define** macro defines constant value and can be any of the basic data types.
- It is used to assign names to different constants or statements which are to be used repeatedly in a program. These defined values or statement can be used by main or in the user defined functions as well. They are used for:
  1. defining a constant,
  2. defining a statement, and
  3. defining a mathematical expression.

- #define directive defines an identifier and a character that will be substituted for the identifier each time it is encountered in the source file.

Syntax:	#define	macro-name	value
	↓	↓	↓
	Macro definition	Macro template	Macro expansion

Program 7.1: Program for macro processor directory.

```
#include <stdio.h>
#define height 100
#define number 3.14
#define letter 'A'
#define letter_sequence "ABC"
#define backslash_char '\?'
void main()
{
  printf("value of height: %d \n", height );
  printf("value of number: %f \n", number );
  printf("value of letter: %c \n", letter );
  printf("value of letter_sequence: %s \n", letter_sequence);
  printf("value of backslash_char: %c \n", backslash_char);
  getch();
}
```

Output:
```
value of height: 100
value of number: 3.140000
value of letter: A
value of letter_sequence: ABC
value of backslash_char:?
```

- Macro substitution statement replaces the macro-name with the given value wherever it appears from the first blank after the macro-name to the end of the file.

Example:

Program	Explanation	Program	Explanation
| ```
/* Program without macros */
#include<stdio.h>
main( )
{
float r=9.5,
area,
pi-3.14
area=pi*r*r;;
printf("\n%f",
area);
pi=8
area = pi*r*r;
printf("\n%f",
area);
}
``` | Here, the value of pi changes from 3.14 to 8. But if user want to keep the value constant throughout the program, then he/she can do this using macros by #define directive. User can also call this as symbolic constant. | ```
/* Program using Macros */
#include<stdio.h>
#define pi 3.14
main( )
{
float r=9.5,
area;
area = pi*r*r;
printf("\n%f",
area);
float pi=8;
area = pi*r*r;
printf("\n%f",
area);
}
``` | #define pi 3.14 macro tells the program to replace the macros pi with value 3.14 where ever it occurs in the program. Thus, C preprocessor writes 3.14 in place of pi. Later on, even if we write pi = 8; the value doesn't change. Instead, it gives error. |

7.4 File Inclusion Directives

- #include directive tells the compiler to read another source file in addition to the one that contains the #include directive.
- The file inclusion directive is beings with #include. The include directive is used to include files like as we include header files in the beginning of the program using #include directive like #include<stdio.h> and #include<conio.h>.
- We have used #include directive in programs written so far.

    #include filename

- The contents of the file given by filename are replaced at the point where the directive is written.
- If we have written number of functions for specific purposes and if we write programs that use them, then declarations of these functions, macros used, declaration of external variables can all be combined in the header file. Instead of repeating the above mentioned statements in each program that uses them, we can include the header file in our programs using the file inclusion directive.
- The header file **stdio.h** supplied with 'C' contains function declarations and all the information regarding input and output. Hence, when we use input/output functions in our programs, we include this header file.

- The file inclusion statement can be written in two ways:
  1. #include "file-name"
     OR
  2. #include <file-name>
- If we use the first way, 'C' would search for the file; filename in the current working directory as well as the specified list of directories.
- If we use the second way, the file; filename will be searched only in the specified list of directories.

  For example: #include<stdio.h>
  #include<string.h>
  #include<conio.h>
- The extension of the include file need not be always '.h' but it can be 'C' also. But **main()** should be in the program and not in the included file.

7.5 Conditional Compilation Directives

- Several directives that allows you to selectively compile portions of your program's source code, this process is known as conditional compilation.
- The preprocessor provides may directives such as #ifdef, #if, #elif, #undef, #ifndef and so on which help you write code which can be compiled depending on the conditions stated.

1. **#if and #elif:**

   The **if** directive tests the expression following it and depending upon the result of the expression decides whether to compile statements.

   Syntax: #if   <conditional-expression>
   　　　　　　　　　　statement 1
   　　　　　　　　　　.............
   　　　　　　　　　　statement n
   　　　　　　　　#else
   　　　　　　　　　　statement 1
   　　　　　　　　　　.............
   　　　　　　　　　　statement m
   　　　　　　　　# endif

Program 7.2: Program to illustrate #if and #elif.
```
#include<stdio.h>
#define PI 3.142
void main()
{
#if PI == 3.142
    printf("The value of PI = % .3f", PI);
#else
    printf("PI value does not defined as 3.142");
#endif
getch();
}
```
Output:
The value of PI = 3.142

- If we have number of conditions to check, instead of using #else or #if number of times, we can use #elif.

    Syntax: #if <condition 1>
    ....
    #elif <condition 2>
    ....
    ....
    #elif <condition n>
    ....
    #else
    ....
    #endif

Program 7.3: Program to illustrate nested #if and #elif.
```
#include<stdio.h>
#define adapter MA
void main()
{
   #if        adapter == MA
              printf("Code for monochrome display");
   #elif      adapter == CGA
              printf("Code for color graphics adapter");
   #elif      adapter = EGA
              printf("Code for enhanced graphics adapter");
   #elif      adapter = VGA
              printf("Code for video graphics adapter");
   #else
              printf("Code for super video graphics adapter");
   #endif
getch();
}
```
Output:
Code for monochrome display

2. **#ifdef:** The #ifdef checks whether, a particular macroname is defined or not. If that macro is already defined, then, you can specify what to compile and execute.

    Syntax:
        #ifdef <macro-name>
            statement 1;
            statement 2;
            ....
            ....
            statement n;
        #endif

- #ifdef and #endif can be used to compile and run debugging code in the program. Debugging of the program requires many values to be displayed on the screen. But after debugging, code is not useful. To erase the code from the program, the option is to use the conditional compilation mechanism like '#ifdef'.

    Syntax: #define debug 1
    ```
    main()
    {
    .........
    .........
    #ifdef debug
            /* put debugging code here */
    #endif
    .........
    .........
    }
    ```
- After debugging is over, the final code need not contain machine code for the display statements as they were required only for checking the program logic at the time of debugging.

Program 7.4: Write a program to illustrate use of #ifdef.

```
#include<stdio.h>
#define display
void main()
{
    int b = 20;
    clrscr();
    b = b + 1;
    #ifdef   display /* if macro 'display' defined */
            printf("b =%d",b);
    #endif
    getch();
}
```

Output:

b = 21

3. **#ifndef:** The #ifndef takes action if the macro name is not defined.

    Syntax: #ifndef <macro-name>
                    statement 1;
                    statement 2;
                    ....
                    statement n;
              #else
                    statement 1;
                    ....
                    ....
                    statement n
              #endif

Program 7.5: Write a program to illustrate use of #ifndef.
```
#include<stdio.h>
/* macro named 'display' is not defined */
void main()
{
   int b = 20;
   b = b + 10;
#ifndef display
   printf("The macro 'display' is not defined");
#else
   printf("b = %d",b);
#endif
getch();
}
```
Output:
```
The macro 'display' is not defined
```

4. **#undef:** The 'undef' means 'undefined'. A macro can be undefined using the #undef directives. It removes the previously made definition to a particular name.

    Syntax:
            #undef <name>

    After the definition of the required name has been removed, it can be redefined using '#define'.

Program 7.6: Write a program to use #undef directive.
```
#include<stdio.h>
#define pi 3.14
void main()
{
   clrscr();
   #if      pi == 3.142
            printf("The value of pi = %.3f",pi);
   #else
            #undef pi      /* remove the definition of 'pi' */
            #define pi 3.142 /* redefine 'pi' */
            printf("The modified value of pi = %.3f",pi);
   #endif
   getch();
}
```
Output:
```
The modified value of pi = 3.142.
```

5. **#pragma:** These are special purpose directives that you can use to turn ON or OFF certain features. There are different pragmas for different compilers. Turbo C compiler has got a pragma, which allows us to write assembly language statements in 'C' program.
- **#Pragma inline:** The #pragma inline is used to tell the 'C' compiler that the code contains the inline assembly statements. 'C' compiler deals with the conversion of 'C' code to machine code. When it finds this directive, it switches over to Turbo assembly code and returns to 'C' code when assembly code ends.

  Syntax:
  ```
  #pragma inline
  asm
  {
     assembly statement 1;
     assembly statement 2;
     ........................
     assembly statement n;
  }
  ```

6. **'#pragma startup' and '#pragma exit':** The '#pragma startup allows to specify functions at starting i.e. before main() is called or upon program exit.

   Syntax: `#pragma startup <function name>`

   and similarly for '#pragma exit' is,

   `#pragma exit <function name>`

   where, the <function name> must be a previously declared function that takes no arguments and returns 'void'. It should be declared as,

   `void <function name> (void)`

Program 7.7: Program to illustrate use of '#pragma startup' and '#pragma exit'.

```
#include<stdio.h>
void start (void);
void end (void);
#pragma    startup    start
#pragma    exit end
void main()
{
   printf("\n Program of pragma directives");
   {
   void start (void)
   {
   printf("Program of start \n");
   }
   void end (void)
   {
   printf("Program of end");
   }
```

Questions

1. Define C preprocessor.
2. With the neat diagram explain working of preprocessor directives.
3. Enlist different preprocessor directives.
4. Describe file inclusion directives.
5. What is meant by conditional compilation? Explain any two of them.
6. Explain macro substitution directive in detail.

Chapter **8**...

File Handling

Contents ...

8.1 Introduction
8.2 Defining and Opening a File
    8.2.1 Defining a File
    8.2.2 Opening a File
    8.2.3 Closing a File
8.3 Standard Functions
8.4 Random Access to Files
8.5 Command Line Arguments
- Questions

8.1 Introduction

- We have taken input from the user and displayed output on the screen. i.e. we have considered console I/O.
- Many applications require that information be stored permanently and it should be possible to access and alter the information whenever necessary.
- In such cases information can be stored in files. 'C' provides a number of functions for using files.
- Files are divided basically in two types:
  1. Stream-oriented (Standard or high-level), and
  2. System-oriented (or low-level)
- Stream oriented data files are easier to work with then are system-oriented data-files and are thus more commonly used.
- Number of library functions are used to operate on files which are broadly classified as:
  1. High level file I/O functions, and
  2. Low level file I/O functions.
- High level file I/O functions do their own buffer management whereas in low level file I/O functions buffer management has to be done by the programmer.
- A buffer is a block of memory where the data to be stored in file is placed temporarily.
- All C language I/O operations is done with streams.
- A stream is a sequence of bytes of data.

- The sequence of bytes of data flowing into a program is an input stream and the flowing into out is output stream.
- C provides following streams:
  1. **stdin:** This is standard input stream, (opened for input).
  2. **stdout:** This is a standard output stream, (opened for output).
  3. **stderr:** This is a standard error stream, (opened for output).

8.2 Defining and Opening a File

8.2.1 Defining a File

- File is a collection of information stored in the secondary memory, having some filename, which is stored in the directory.

OR

- File is a set of instructions.
- File is not opening, before opening a file we need to establish a file pointer.
    ```
    FILE * fptr;
    ```
- FILE is a structure defined in the header file, "stdio.h".
- This header files stores all the information regarding the file i.e. name of the file, in what mode it is opened, starting buffer address, a character pointer which points to the character being read. The above statement establishes a buffer area. Each file opening has its own file structure. Before processing any file, it must be opened.

8.2.2 Opening a File

- On opening a file link is established between the program and the operating system through the FILE structure, since, operating system returns a pointer to the structure FILE.
- Opening a file associates the file name with buffer area. The fopen () function opens a file whose name is pointed to by 'filename' and returns the stream that is associated with it.
- The file opening function is written as:

    ```
    fopen (file-name, file-type);
    ```
    where,   file-name = Name of data file to be opened

    file-type = Mode or manner in which data will be used (i.e. whether for reading, writing etc.)

File Handling

- The different modes in which the file can be opened are:

Mode	Meaning
"r"	Open a text file for reading
"w"	Create a text file for writing
"a"	Append to a text file
"rb"	Open a binary file for reading
"wb"	Create a binary file for writing
"ab"	Append to a binary file
"rt"	Open a text file for read/write
"wt"	Create a text file for read/write
"at"	Open or create a text file for read/write
"r + b"	Open a binary file for read/write
"w + b"	Create a binary file for read/write
"a + b"	Open or create binary file for read/write
"rt"	Open a text file for reading
"wt"	Create a text file for writing
"at"	Append to a text file
"r + t"	Open a text file for read/write
"w + t"	Create a text file for read/write
"a + t"	Open or create a text file for read/write

- **Important points to remember while selecting modes:**
    1. When the mode is "writing (w)" a file with the specified name is created if the file does not exist. If the file already exists, the contents are deleted and the file is opened a fresh.
    2. When the purpose is 'appending', the file is opened with the current contents safe. A file with the specified name is created if the file does not exist.
    3. If the purpose is "reading", and if it exists then the file is opened with the current contents same. If the file does not exist, it creates an error.
    4. r + the existing file is opened to the beginning for both reading and writing.
    5. w + Same as w except both reading and writing.
    6. a + Same as a except both for reading and writing.
- From the above explanations, it is expected the above table would be clear.

Examples:
```
file *f1, *f2;
f1 = fopen ("data", "w");
f2 = fopen ("input", "r");
```
We can open any number of files at a time.

8.2.3 Closing a File

- It is necessary that when in the program a file is opened then it should be closed as soon as the work with the file is over or atleast at the end of program.
- This ensures that all outstanding information associated with the file is flushed out from the buffers and all links to the file are broken. It also prevents any accidental misuse of the file. Also we have to close the file if we want to open the same file in a different mode.

Syntax:
```
fclose (file-pointer);
    OR
fclose all();
```

For example:
```
FILE *p1, *p2;
p1 = fopen ("input", "r");
p2 = fopen ("output", "w");
_____

_____
fclose (p1);
fclose (p2);
```

- The syntax for closing the file is same, irrespective of the mode in which it is opened.

End of File (feof( )):

- Sometimes, we do not know how big the file is. To detect end of file we use feof();
- In text files, a special character EOF denotes the end of file. End-of-File can be detected, as soon as this character is read. In binary files, the EOF is not there.

Syntax:
```
feof(file_pointer);
```

For example:
```
while (! feof (fptr))
{
    _____
    _____
    _____
}
```

Program 8.1: C program to illustrate how to file stored on the disk is read.

```c
#include<stdio.h>
#include<stdlib.h>
void main()
{
   FILE *ptr;
   char filename[15];
   char ch;
   printf("Enter the filename to be opened \n");
   scanf("%s", filename);
   /* open the file for reading */
   ptr = fopen(filename, "r");
   if(ptr == NULL)
   {
      printf("Cannot open file \n");
      exit(0);
   }
   ch = fgetc(ptr);
   while(ch!=EOF)
   {
      printf("%c", ch);
      ch = fgetc(ptr);
   }
   fclose(ptr);
}
```

8.3 Standard Functions

- Before using any file it is necessary to create the file. It can be created by,
    1. Using any text editor directly, and
    2. By writing a program, to write into the file.
- Program will consist of accepting character input from user and writing to the file using file processing function 'fputc'. Any existing file or file created in the above manner can be read in any of the following way:
    1. Directly by using operating system commands, such as print or type.
    2. Using the text editor or word processor.
    3. A program can be written to read the file.

- In the program function fgetc( ) reads characters from data file and putchar( ) will display them on the screen. Individual data characters can also be processed as they are read.
- Thus, fputc( ) is a function used to write data character in a file.

    int fputc (int ch, FILE *ptvar)
    ch = character to be written
    ptvar = File pointer

- fgetc( ) is the counterpart of the function fputc, and it is used to read a character from the file. It returns the character read to the calling program.

    int fgetc (FILE * ptvar)

1. **getc( ) and putc( ) Functions:**
- These are the simplest input/output functions used for files. With these we can put in and get out a single character from a file.
- To use a putc function it is necessary that the file must be opened in writing mode. It is similar to puts ( ) function. The fopen () function opens a file whose name is pointed to by 'filename' and returns the stream that is associated with it.
- The difference is that putc can only put a single character. The similarity is puts put a string on screen and putc( ) puts a character in file.
- The **general format of putc( )** is,

    putc (c, fp1)

    where c is a character and

    fp1 is a file pointer.

- The fgetc() function returns the next character from the specified input stream and increments the file position indicator. The character is read as an unsigned char that is converted to an integer. If the end-of-file is reached, fgetc() returns EOF. If fgetc() encounters an error, EOF is also returned.
- The **general format of getc()**,

    getc (fp2)

    where, fp2 is a file pointer which is already opened in reading mode.

- When a file is opened the file pointer is set to the beginning of the file - when we perform certain operation in the file the pointer points to some variable address.
- Whereas, when a file is closed the compiler automatically puts a EOF mark. This determines the end of file. Again if the file is opened the pointer marks to the beginning of file.
- To stop inputting data or to close the file we can use ^z [control z] at the end of input. This will close the file.

Program 8.2: Program to demonstrate file input/output.

```
#include<stdio.h>
#include<conio.h>
void main()
{
    FILE *f1;
    char c;
    clrscr();
    printf("Data Input\n\n");
    f1 = fopen("INPUT", "w")
    while((c=getchar()) ! = EOF)
    putc(c, f1);
    fclose(f1);
    printf("\nData Output\n\n");
    f1 = fopen("INPUT", "r");
    while((c=getc(f1)) !=EOF)
        printf("%c", c);
    fclose(f1);
    getch():
```

2. getw( ) and putw( ) Functions:

- These are similar to the getc( ) and putc( ) function. The only difference is with this we can read and write on integer or numeric quantity from the file.
- The **general formats** are:

    putw (integer, fp);

    And

    getw (fp);

    where, fp is the file pointer.

- For this purpose we choose 3 different files. In the first file first we store the list. We close the file and open it again in reading mode. At the same time we open two different files odd and even in writing mode.

- We read an int from first file and find whether it is even or odd. We put it in corresponding file. Then we close all the file and then open odd and even in reading mode. We just read the files and display the contents on screen.

Program 8.3: Program to demonstrate files.

```
#include<stdio.h>
#include<stdlib.h>
main ()
{
   file *fp1, *fp2, *fp3;
   int i,no;
   clrscr();
   fp1=fopen("input","w");
   printf("please enter the list and enter - 1 to end:");
   do
   {
      scanf("%d",&no);
      if (no == -1)
      break;
      else
      putw (no,fp1);
   }while(1);
   fclose(fp1);
   fp1=fopen("input","r");
   fp2=fopen("odd","w");
   fp3=fopen("even","w");
   do
   {
      no=getw(fp1);
      if(no==EOF)
      break;
      else
      {
              if(no%2==0)
              put(no,fp3);
              else
              putw(no,fp2);
      }
   } while(1);
```

```c
        fcloseall();
        fp1=fopen("even","r");
        fp2=fopen("odd","r");
        printf("\nTHE EVEN NUMBERS ARE:");
        do
        {
           no=getw(fp1);
           if(no==EOF)
           break;
           else
           printf("\n%d",no);
        } while(1);
        fclose(fp1);
        printf("\nTHE CONTENTS OF ODD FILE ARE:");
        do
        {
           no=getw(fp2);
           if(no==EOF)
            break;
           else
           printf("%\nd",no);
        }while(1);
        fcloseall();
        getch();
    }
```

Output:
```
    Please enter the list and enter - 1 to end:
    1 2 3 4 5 6 7 8 9 10 – 1
    The constants of even file are
    2
    4
    6
    8
    10
    The contents of odd file are
    1
    3
    5
    7
    9
```

- So we have demonstrated a programme which utilizes file functions.

3. fprintf( ) and fscanf( ) Functions:

- These are similar to printf( ) and scanf( ) functions in a single way.
   - **(i) printf( ):** function writes on the screen and fprintf( ) writes in the file.
   - **(ii) scanf( ):** function reads from the standard i/p device and fscanf( ) reads data from the file.
- The fprintf() function outputs the values of the arguments that makes up the argument list as specified in the format string to the stream pointed to by stream. The operations of the format control string and command are identical to those in printf().
- The **general format of fprint** is,

   i.e.   `fprintf (fp, "control string", list)`

   OR

   `fprintf (pointer name, "control string", argument)`

   where fp is the file pointer. The control string contains output specifications for the items in the list. The list may include variables constants and strings.

   `fprintf (fp1, "%d %s %d", mark,s name, roll);`
- The fscanf function works exactly like the scanf function except that it reads the information from the stream specified by stream instead of standard input device.
- The **general format of fscanf function is**,

   i.e. `fscanf(fp, "control string", list);`

   OR

   `fscanf(ptr, "control string", list);`
- This will read elements from the file specified by the pointer fp, according to specifications contained in the control string.

   For example:

   `fscanf (fp, "%s %d", name, & phno);`

   These functions are much comparable to the ordinary printf and scanf functions. If the end of file is reached, fscanf ( ) returns a EOF value.

   With the functions in order to put input or get output from a file we have to use functions stdin and stdout we will consider the explanation after the following example.

Program 8.4: Program to demonstrate fprintf( ) and fscanf( ) functions.

```
#include<stdio.h>
#include<stdlib.h>
main()
{
   FlLE *fp1;
   int phno,wt,ht,n,i;
   char name[30], filename[20];
```

```
    printf ("Input filename");
    scanf ("%s", filename);
    fp1 = fopen (filename, "w");
    printf ("How many no. of i/p:");
    scanf("%d", &n);
    for(i=0;i<n; i ++)
    {
        fscanf (stdin, "%s %d %d", name, &phno, &wt, &ht);
        fprintf (fp1, "%s %d %d", name, phno, wt, ht);
    }
    fclose (fp1);
    printf ("\n \n");
    fp1 = fopen (filename, "r");
    printf ("\n Name \t phno \t wt \t ht");
    for(i=0;i<n;i++)
    {
        fscanf (fp1, "%s %d %d %d", name, &phno, &wt, &ht);
        fprintf (stdout, "%s \t %d \t %d \t %d, name, phno, wt, ht);
    }
        fclose all ();
}                /* end of main */
```

Output:

Input file name:
Mangala stores.
How many number of records in i/p: 2
    Deepak   62119   60   5.8
    Sachin   459520   62   5.7

- Now whatever is to be written in file is gives form the keyboard. Data is read using the function fscanf( ) from the file stdin, which refers to the terminal and then it is written to the file pointed by the file pointer fp1.
- When the file is opened in reading mode, the data from the file along with the item values are written to the file stdout, which refers to the screen. While reading from a file care should be taken to use the same format specification with which the constants have been written to the file.

4. fgets( ) and fputs( ) Functions:

- These are similar to the gets( ) and puts( ) function. These functions are useful to input and output strings from the file.

- The fgets() function reads up to num-1character from stream and store them into a character array pointed to by str. Characters are read until either a newline or an EOF is received or until the specified limit is reached. After the character has been read, a null is stored in the array immediately after the last character is read. A newline character will be retained and will be a part of the array pointed to by str.
- If successful, fgets() returns str; a null pointer is returned upon failure. If a read error occurs, the content of the array pointed to by str are indeterminate.
- The **standard format for fgets()** is:
    ```
    fputs(cont char *str, file *fp)
    ```
    i.e.
    ```
    fputs(string to be inputted, file pointer)
    ```
- The fputs() function writes the content of the string pointed to by str to the specified stream. The null terminator is not written. The fputs() function returns non negative on success and EOF on failure.
- The **format for fputs()** is:
    ```
    fgets (char *str, int length, file *fp)
    ```
    i.e.
    ```
    fgets (string, string length, file pointer);
    ```
- The fgets( ) function reads a string from the specified stream until either a new line character or length (– 1) characters have been read. If a new line is read, it will be part of the string. However, fgets( ) is terminated, the resultant string will be null terminated.

5. fread() and fwrite() Functions:

- With the help of these command's reading and writing of blocks of data can be done. The standard format is:

    Syntax for fread() is:
    ```
    size_t fread (void *buffer, size_t num_bytes, size_t count, file fp)
    ```
    Syntax for fwrite() is:
    ```
    size_t fwrite (const void *buffer, size_t num-bytes, size_t count, file *fp);
    ```
    where

    const void buffer is the variable name or array name or structure variable name which is to be written in the file.

    size-t num-bytes is the no. of bytes which the input or output data is expected to occupy.

    size-t count keeping the above no. of bytes in consideration, the no. of such elements which require above specified memory.
    ```
    file *fp → file pointer
    ```
    (i) For example:
    ```
    fwrite (& rec1 [i], sizeof (rec1 [0]), 1, fp1)
    ```
    (ii) For example:
    ```
    fwrite (& rec1, size of (rec1 [0]), n, fp1)
    ```

- The first example (i) tells the compiler to write array element rec1 [1], and the size of it is given by size occupied by rec1 [0]. Only one element is to be written and at last is the file pointer.
- In the second example (ii) we want to write an whole array having n elements in the file. So first we write array name with an ambersand '&' sign, and we have to store 'n' array elements each of size (rec1 [0] i.e. on single array element). So we give size command and at last is the file pointer.

For example:

fwrite (&f, sizeof (float), 1, fp)).

This declaration of size is also considered as valid. Suppose, we want to write a whole array balance in the file we can write it as,

fwrite (balance, sizeof (balance, 1, fp));

From the above explanation is quite simple to understand this declaration. As in size we are write, where array, so further we give only '1'.

For fread also all the above declaration holds good, the only difference is we do not have to use the ambersand (&) sign.

For example:

fread (balance, size of balance, 1, fp);

where balance is an array.

Program 8.5: Program to write a structure element in a file and print it.

```
#include<stdio.h>
struct record
{
char customer_name[80];
int ph_no;
}customer[10];
void main()
{
   FILE *fp;
   int n,i;
   flushall();
   fp=fopen("input","w");
   clrscr();
   printf("HOW MANY RECORD TO BE FILLED:");
   scanf("%d",&n);
```

```
        for(i=0;i<n;i++)
        {
           printf("\nPLEASE ENTER CUSTOMER NAME:");
           scanf("%s", customer[i].customer_name);
           printf("\nPLEASE ENTER PHONE NO.:");
           scanf("%d",&customer[i].ph_no);
           fwrite(&customer[i],sizeof(customer[0]),1,fp);
        }
        fcloseall();
        fp=fopen("input","r");
        printf("\nCUSTOMER NAME \tCUSTOMER PHONE NO.\n");
        for(i=0;i<n;i++)
        {
           fread(&customer[i],sizeof(customer[0]),1,fp);
    printf("\n%s\t%d",customer[i].customer_name,customer[i].ph_no);
        }
        getch();
     }
```

Output:
```
     How many records to be filled: 2
     Please enter customer name: Neelam Enterprises
     Please enter ph_no: 628119
     Please enter customer name: Modern arts
     Please enter ph_no: 661916
     Customer name              Phone no.
     Neelam Enterprises         628119
     Modern Arts                661916
```

6. **Error Handling Input/Output Operations:**
- While dealing with files, if some error occurs then it is difficult to detect the error. So we should take care while writing the programs only.
- Typical error situations include:
    (i) Trying to read beyond the end-of-file mark.
    (ii) Device overflows.
    (iii) Trying to use a file that has not been opened.
    (iv) Trying to perform an operation on a file, when the file is opened for another type of operation.
    (v) Opening a file with invalid filename.
    (vi) Attempting to write to a write-protected file.

- Also to check of success of our command C provides us certain checks.
- We can check the end of file condition by the following command,
    ```
    if (feof (fp))
    printf ("end of data")
    ```
- This feof( ) functions returns a nonzero integer value if all of the data from the specified file has been read, and returns zero otherwise.
- ferror() function determines whether a file operation has produced an error.
- ferror() has following prototype:
    ```
    int ferror(file *fp);
    ```
- The ferror function reports the status of the file indicated. It takes FILE pointer as its argument and returns a non-zero integer if an error has been detected upto that point, during processing. It returns zero otherwise.
    ```
    If (ferror (fp) = 0)
    printf ("An error has occurred");
    ```
    we can check whether a file is properly opened or not by this command,
    ```
    if (fp = = NULL)
    printf (" File could not be opened");
    ```

8.4 Random Access to Files

- In the beginning we had considered about some functions. Now, we try to study and understand those functions one by one.

1. ftell( ) Function:
- This function just tells us the relative position of pointer (in bytes) i.e. number of bytes written in the file.
- This function tells where the pointer is positioned right now. It returns this pointer as a long integer which is an offset from the beginning of the file. returns – 1L on error
    ```
    long ftell(FILE * fp);
    ```
    For example: n = ftell (fp)
    So fp is a file pointer and the value of bytes will be stored in n.n should be an integer.

2. rewind( ) Function:
- This function is used when the file is opened in append mode. This will again reset the pointer to the beginning of the file.
- This function places the pointer to the beginning of the file, irrespective of where it is present right now.
    ```
    void rewind(FILE * fp);
    ```
    For example: rewind (fp)
    where fp is a file pointer. So file pointer will be set to beginning of file.
    For example: rewind (fp);
    ```
              n = ftell (fp);
    ```

- So n will be assigned a value 0. An important point to note, the first byte in file is numbered as 0, second as 1 and so on. This function helps us to read and write a file or read the file more than one, without having to close and open the file.

3. fseek( ) Function:
- With this function we can move the file pointer to a desired position.
- **General format is:**

        fseek (file ptr, offset, position)

    where first parameter is the file pointer. Offset is number or variable of type long, and position is an int number. The offset specifies the number of positions (bytes) to be moved from the location specified by position. The position can have 3 values,

Macro name	Value	Meaning
SEEK_SET	0	Beginning of file
SEEK_CUR	1	Current position
SEER_END	2	End of file

For example:

fseek(fptr, 0, SEEK_END); This positions the pointer to end of the line.

Program 8.6: Program to reverse a file using fseek( ).

```
#include<stdio.h>
main()
{
    typedef struct {
            char name[10];
            int emp_no;
            int salary;
            }record;
    record emp;
    FILE *fs, *ft;
    long recsize;
    int k, n;
    long lCurrentPos;
    int bIsEOF = 0;
        recsize = sizeof(emp);
        fs = fopen("c:\\test\\recordb.dat","r");
        ft = fopen("c:\\test\\recordbr.dat","w");
        fseek(fs,-recsize,SEEK_END);
        fseek(ft,0,SEEK_SET);
```

```c
    do
    {
       k = fread (&emp, recsize, 1, fs);
       printf("\nK read = %d",k);
       n = fwrite(&emp, recsize, 1, ft);
       printf("\nN written = %d"n);
       lCurrentPos = ftell( fs );
       if ( lCurrentPos == recsize )
       {
            if ( bIsEOF )
            {
               /*All file is parsed reached at the end of record */
               break;
            }
            fseek(fs, — (recsize), SEEK_cuR);
/* This is last record which is going to write in the file so next loop we will break after writing this record for this make flag to true */
         bIsEOF = 1;
       }
       else
       {
            fseek(fs,- (2*recsize),SEEK_CUR);
       }
    }while(lCurrentPos);

 fclose(fs);
 fclose(ft);
 }
```

Programs

Program 1: Program to open a file.
```
 #include <stdio.h>
 #include <stdlib.h>
 int main()
 {
  char ch, file_name[25];
  FILE *fp;
  printf("Enter the name of file you wish to see\n");
  gets(file_name);
```

```c
    fp = fopen(file_name,"r"); // read mode
    if( fp == NULL )
    {
    perror("Error while opening the file.\n");
    exit(EXIT_FAILURE);
    }
    printf("The contents of %s file are:\n", file_name);
    while( ( ch = fgetc(fp) ) != EOF )
    printf("%c",ch);

    fclose(fp);
    return 0;
    }
```

Output:
```
Enter the name of file you wish to see
computerprogramming.txt
The contents of computerprogramming.txt file are:
Computer programming is fun.
```

Program 2: Program to copy files.
```c
    #include <stdio.h>
    #include <stdlib.h>
    int main()
    {
     char ch, source_file[20], target_file[20];
     FILE *source, *target;
     printf("Enter name of file to copy\n");
     gets(source_file);
     source = fopen(source_file, "r");
     if( source == NULL )
     {
     printf("Press any key to exit...\n");
     exit(EXIT_FAILURE);
     }
     printf("Enter name of target file\n");
     gets(target_file);
     target = fopen(target_file, "w");
```

```
    if( target == NULL )
    {
    fclose(source);
    printf("Press any key to exit...\n");
    exit(EXIT_FAILURE);
    }
    while( ( ch = fgetc(source) ) != EOF )
    fputc(ch, target);
    printf("File copied successfully.\n");
    fclose(source);
    fclose(target);
    return 0;
    }
```
Output:
```
    Enter name of file to copy
    factorial.c
    Enter name of target file
    factorial_copy.c
    File copied successfully.
```
Program 3: Program to merge files.
```
    #include <stdio.h>
    #include <stdlib.h>
    int main()
    {
     FILE *fs1, *fs2, *ft;
     char ch, file1[20], file2[20], file3[20];
     printf("Enter name of first file\n");
     gets(file1);
     printf("Enter name of second file\n");
     gets(file2);
     printf("Enter name of file which will store contents of two files\n");
     gets(file3);
     fs1 = fopen(file1,"r");
     fs2 = fopen(file2,"r");
```

```c
        if( fs1 == NULL || fs2 == NULL )
        {
        perror("Error ");
        printf("Press any key to exit...\n");
        getch();
        exit(EXIT_FAILURE);
        }
        ft = fopen(file3,"w");
        if( ft == NULL )
        {
        perror("Error ");
        printf("Press any key to exit...\n");
        exit(EXIT_FAILURE);
        }
        while( ( ch = fgetc(fs1) ) != EOF )
        fputc(ch,ft);
        while( ( ch = fgetc(fs2) ) != EOF )
        fputc(ch,ft);
        printf("Two files were merged into %s file successfully.\n",file3);
        fclose(fs1);
        fclose(fs2);
        fclose(ft);
        return 0;
        }
```

Output:

```
Enter name of first file
date.c
Enter name of second file
factorial.c
Enter name of file which will store contents of two files
date-factorial.c
Two files were merged into date-factorial.c file successfully
```

Program 4: Program to delete a file.
```c
#include<stdio.h>
main()
{
 int status;
 char file_name[25];
 printf("Enter the name of file you wish to delete\n");
 gets(file_name);
 status = remove(file_name);
 if( status == 0 )
 printf("%s file deleted successfully.\n",file_name);
 else
 {
 printf("Unable to delete the file\n");
 perror("Error");
 }
 return 0;
}
```
Output:
```
Enter the name of file you wish to delete
leap-year.c
leap-year.c file delete successfully.
```

Program 5: Copy text from one file to other file.
```c
#include<stdio.h>
#include<conio.h>
#include<stdlib.h>
void main()
{
 FILE *fp1,*fp2;
 char ch;
 clrscr();
 fp1 = fopen("Sample.txt","r");
 fp2 = fopen("Output.txt","w");
 while(1)
 {
 ch = fgetc(fp1);
```

```
        if(ch==EOF)
        break;
        else
        putc(ch,fp2);
        }
        printf("File copied succesfully!");
        fclose(fp1);
        fclose(fp2);
        }
```

Output:
```
    File copied successfully!
```

Explanation: To copy a text from one file to another we have to follow following Steps:

Step 1: Open Source File in Read Mode
```
    fp1 = fopen("Sample.txt","r");
```
Step 2: Open Target File in Write Mode
```
    fp2 = fopen("Output.txt","w");
```
Step 3: Read Source File Character by Character
```
    while(1)
      {
      ch = fgetc(fp1);

      if(ch==EOF)
      break;
      else
      putc(ch,fp2);
      }
```

- "fgetc" will read character from source file.
- Check whether character is "End Character of File" or not, if yes then Terminate Loop.
- "putc" will write Single Character on File Pointed by "fp2" pointer.

Input Text File:
    C Programming is very funny language

Output Written on File
    C Programming is very funny language

Program 6: Program to convert the file contents in upper-case and write contents in a output file.

```c
#include <stdio.h>
struct complex
{
 int real, img;
};
int main()
{
 struct complex a, b, c;
 printf("Enter a and b where a + ib is the first complex number.\n");
 printf("a = ");
 scanf("%d", &a.real);
 printf("b = ");
 scanf("%d", &a.img);
 printf("Enter c and d where c + id is the second complex number.\n");
 printf("c = ");
 scanf("%d", &b.real);
 printf("d = ");
 scanf("%d", &b.img);
 c.real = a.real + b.real;
 c.img = a.img + b.img;
 if ( c.img >= 0 )
 printf("Sum of two complex numbers = %d + %di\n",c.real,c.img);
 else
 printf("Sum of two complex numbers = %d %di\n",c.real,c.img);
 return 0;
}
```

Output:
```
Enter a and b where a + ib is the first complex number.
a = 3
b = 4
Enter c and d where c + id is the second complex number.
c = 2
d = 1
Sum of two complex numbers = 5 + 5i
```

Program 7: Program for display line by line the contents.
```c
#include<stdio.h>
#include<conio.h>
int main(argc,argv)
int argc;
char *argv[];
{
   FILE *fp;
   char ch[100];
   int loop=0;
   if(argc!=2)
   {
 printf("usage is wrong");
       return;
   }
   fp=fopen(argv[1],"r");
   if(fp==NULL)
   {
     printf("file opening error");
     return;
   }
   printf("string\n");
for(loop=0,ch[loop]=getc(fp);feof(fp)==0;loop++,ch[loop]=getc(fp))
   {
     if(ch[loop]=='\n')
     {
      ch[++loop]='\0';
      printf("%s",ch);
      loop=-1;
     }
   }
 ch[loop]='\0';
   printf("%s",ch);
   fcloseall();
    getch();
}
```

8.5 Command Line Arguments

- Command line is a line on which we are able to provide arguments to program. To see the command line just type and in run option of start option of desktop of computer, as select start → select run → type and you see C:\> .... this dotted line is called as commercial line.
- It is possible to pass some values from the command line to you C programs when they are executed. These values are called command line arguments and many times they are important for you program specially when you want to control your program from outside instead of hard coding those values inside the code.
- Declaration of main looks like this:

    int main(int argc, char *argv[])

    where

    argc   number of arguments in the command line including program name, and

    argc[] This is carrying all the arguments.

Program 8.7: Program for command line argument.

```
#include<stdio.h>
#include<stdlib.h>
int main(int argc, char *argv[])   //command line arguments
{
if(argc!=5)
{
printf("Arguments passed through command line not equal to 5");
printf("\n Program name: %s\n", argv[0]);
printf("1st arg : %s\n", argv[1]);
printf("1st arg : %s\n", argv[2]);
printf("1st arg : %s\n", argv[3]);
printf("1st arg : %s\n", argv[4]);
printf("1st arg : %s\n", argv[5]);
return 0;
}
```

Output:

```
Program name: test
1st arg : this
2nd arg: is
3rd arg : a
4th arg : program
5th arg : (null)
```

Program 8.8: Print all arguments passed to C program using command line.

```
#include<stdio.h>
int main(int args, char * argv[])
{
   int i=0;
   for(i=0; i<args; i++)
     printf("\n%s", argv[i]);
   return 0;
}
```

Questions

1. What is file?
2. What is the difference between fscanf( ), fprintf( ) and fread( ), fwrite( )?
3. What is a file pointer and file?
4. Open a file, write the values of:
   int a = 10;
   float b = 13.333;
   char c = 'D';
   in the file and close it.
5. Find out the purpose and use of library functions feof( ).
6. Write a program to remove all blank lines from a file.
7. Explain gets( ) and puts( ) functions.
8. With neat diagram explain following functions:
   (a) rewind( )
   (b) ftell( )
   (c) fseek( )
9. Explain the term fread( ).
10. Explain the term fwrite( ).
11. Explain the term fprintf( ).
12. Explain the term fscanf( ).
13. Write short notes on random access to files.
14. Enlist various operations of a file.
15. Explain the term file pointer.
16. With syntax describe following function:
    (a) sscanf( )
    (b) sprintf( )
17. Explain command line argument with example.

F.Y.B.C.A. (Semester - II)
PROCEDURE ORIENTED PROGRAMMING USING - 'C'
Question Papers

Time : 3 Hours   October 2014   Max. Marks : 80

Q.1 Answers the following (Any Ten):   [10 × 2 = 20]

(a) What is nested structure?
Ans. Refer to Section 3.2.3.
(b) List different types of files.
Ans. Refer to Section 8.1.
(c) Define union with example.
Ans. Refer to Section 6.4.
(d) Explain str(atc) and str(pyc).
Ans. Refer to Section 5.6.
(e) State different types of relational operators in 'C'.
Ans. Refer to Section 1.4.1.
(f) Define Recursion.
Ans. Refer to Section 4.5.
(g) List different preprocessor directives.
Ans. Refer to Sections 7.3, 7.4 and 7.5.
(h) What is formal parameter? Give example.
Ans. Refer to Section 1.4.6.2.
(i) Give syntax and usage of for loop.
Ans. Refer to Section 3.3.1.
(j) What is Identifier?
Ans. Refer to Section 1.4.4.
(k) Define Algorithm.
Ans. Refer to Section 1.1.4.
(l) What is escape sequence?
Ans. Refer to Section 1.4.5.

Q.2 Answers the following (Any Four):   [4 × 5 = 20]

(a) Explain difference between do-while and while loop with example.
Ans. Refer to Sections 3.3.2 and 3.3.3.
(b) Define Array. Explain how to declare and initialize two dimensional array with example.
Ans. Refer to Section 5.1.
(c) Define function and explain function declaration, function definition and function call with example.
Ans. Refer to Sections 4.1 and 4.3.
(d) What is pointer? Explain how to declare and initialize pointer variable with suitable example.
Ans. Refer to Section 4.6.
(e) What is dynamic memory allocation? Explain its advantages.
Ans. Refer to Section 4.9.

Q.3 Answers the following (Any Four): [4 × 5 = 20]

(a) Write a 'C' program for multiplication of m × n matrix.

Ans. Refer to Program 14 of Chapter 5.

(b) Write a 'C' program to check if the given string is palindrome or not.

Ans. Refer to Program 5.28 of Chapter 5.

(c) Create a structure to store data of 10 students as roll no, name and percentage. Write a 'C' program to print roll no, names of students who have succeed less than 60 percent.

Ans. Refer to Program 6.8 of Chapter 6.

(d) Write a 'C' program to calculate the sum of following series using function.
$$\text{Sum} = 1 + \frac{1}{x} + \frac{1}{x^2} + \frac{1}{x^3} + \frac{1}{x^4} \ldots$$

Ans. Refer to Chapter 4.

(e) Write a 'C' program to convert temperature from celcius to faharanite.

Ans. Refer to Section 2, Program 2.8.

Q.4 Trace the output and justify (Any Four): [4 × 5 = 20]

(a)
```
main()
{
    int i = 1;
    for (; ;)
    printf("%d", i);
}
```

Ans. **Output:** Displays 1 infinite times.

(b)
```
main()
{
    Char s[] = "I am the best";
    Printf("%s", s);
    Printf("\n%c", s[3]);
    Printf("\n%c", s[8]);
}
```

Ans. **Output:**   I am the best
            m
            displays space

(c)
```
main()
{
    int x, y, z;
    x = y = z = 1;
    z = + + x || + + y & & + + z;
    printf(" x = % d y = % d z = % d \ n", x, y, z);
}
```

Ans. **Output:** x = 2, y = 1, z = 1.

(d)
```
main()
{
   int i = 0, x = 0;
   for(i = 1; i < 10; i++)
   {
      if(i % 2 == 1)
      x = x + 1;
      else
      x - -;
      printf("% d", x);
   }
};
```
Ans. **Output:** 101010101

(e)
```
main()
{
   int j = 1;
   while()
   {
      printf("% d", j++);
      if(j > 3)
      break;
   }
}
```
Ans. **Output:** Code will display syntax error.

Time : 3 Hours   **April 2015**   **Max. Marks : 80**

Q.1 Answer the following (Any Ten):   [10 × 2 = 20]
 (a) What is Indirection operator.
Ans. Refer to Section 4.7.
 (b) Give syntax to define self Referential structure.
Ans. Refer to Section 6.0.
 (c) Explain strlen() and strcpy().
Ans. Refer to Section 4.2.
 (d) What are the difference types of files?
Ans. Refer to Section 8.0.
 (e) How is a union Declared and Initialized?
Ans. Refer to Section 6.4.
 (f) Define string with an example.
Ans. Refer to Section 5.6.
 (g) Define pointer to pointer.
 (h) What is the significance of argv[0]?
Ans. Refer to Section 8.5.

(i) List primary data type in C language.
Ans. Refer to Section 3.3.
(j) "Size of is an operator in 'c' " state true to false.
Ans. Refer to Section 1.5.
(k) List all Bitwise operator.
Ans. Refer to Section 1.5.
(l) Define structure with an example.
Ans. Refer to Section 6.1.1.

Q.2 Attempt Any Four of the following: [4 × 5 = 20]
(a) What is pointer? Explain Array of pointer in detail.
    (i) Putc() and fputc().
    (ii) fprintf() and fscanf().
Ans. (i) Refer to Section 8.3.
    (ii) Refer to Section 8.3.
(b) Compare Macro with functions.
Ans. Refer to Section 7.3.
(c) What is Dynamic Memory Allocation? Explain functions used to allocate and delete memory dynamically.
Ans. Refer to Section 4.9.
(d) How can Array be passed to function? Explain with example.
Ans. Refer to Section 5.4.
(e) Define recursion. Explain recursion with example.
Ans. Refer to Section 4.5.

Q.3 Attempt Any Four of the following: [4 × 5 = 20]
(a) Write a 'C' program to check if given string is palindrome or not using pointers.
Ans. Refer to Program 5.28 of Chapter 5.
(b) Create structure to store data of 10 employees as employee number, name and salary. Write a 'C' program to print Employee Numbers and names of Employees having salary greater then 10,000.
Ans. Refer to Programs of Chapter 6.
(c) Write a C program to accept a four digit number from user and count zero, odd and even digits of the entered number.
Ans. Refer to Chapters 3 and 5.
(d) Write a 'C' program to accept a string from user and generate following pattern (e.g. input is string "abcd").
a
a b
a b c
a b c d
a b c
a b
a
Ans. Refer to Chapters 3 and 5.
(e) Write a 'C' program to convert upper case to lower case by using file.
Ans. Refer to Program 6 of Chapter 8.

Q.4 Trace the output and justify: [4 × 5 = 20]

(a)
```
Main()
{
    int a[5] = {5, 1, 15, 20, 25};
    int i,j,m;
    i=++a[1];
    j=a[1]++;
    m=a[i++];
    printf("%d %d %d",i,j,m);
    getch();
}
```
Ans. **Output:** 3, 2, 15

(b)
```
#define PRODUCT (x) (x * x)
main()
{
    int i=3,j;
    j=PRODUCT(i + 1);
    printf("\n %d",j);
}
```
Ans. Refer to Chapter 7.

(c)
```
Main()
{
    int i=-5,j=-2;
        junk(i,&j);
    printf("i=%d j=%d\n",i,j);
    junk(int i, int*j)
    {
        i=i*j;
        *j=*j**j;
    }
}
```
Ans. **Output:** Shows syntax error regarding 'use of pointer'.

(d)
```
Main()
{
    char s[]="Aw what the breek";
    printf("%s",s);
    printf("ln%c",s[3]);
    printf("ln%c",s[1]);
}
```
Ans. **Output:** Aw what the breek lnwlnw

(e)
```
Main()
{
    Char s₁[]="FYBCA SYBCA TYBCA";
    Char s₂[20];
    Char s₃[20];
    scanf(s₁,"%s %s %s", s₁,s₂,s₃);
    printf("%s, %s, %s", s₁,s₂,s₃);
}
```
Ans. **Output:** FYBCA   SYBCA   TYBCA , ,

Procedure Oriented Programming using C   P.6   Question Papers

Time : 3 Hours   **November 2015**   **Max. Marks : 80**

1. **Answer the following (Any Ten):**   [10 × 2 = 20]
   1. What is keyword? Explain with example.
   - Ans. Refer to Section 1.4.3.
   2. List all relational operators in 'C'.
   - Ans. Refer to Section 1.5.
   3. Give syntax of scanf statement with example.
   - Ans. Refer to Section 2.2.2.
   4. Usage of getchar() and gets() with example.
   - Ans. Refer to Sections 2.2.3 and 2.3.
   5. What is the use of continue statement. Give example.
   - Ans. Refer to Section 3.4.3.
   6. Define Pointer? Explain with example.
   - Ans. Refer to Section 4.6.
   7. What is two dimensional array? Explain with example.
   - Ans. Refer to Section 5.3.
   8. What is use of calloc function?
   - Ans. Refer to Section 4.9.
   9. Explain strlen() and strcpy().
   - Ans. Refer to Section 5.6.2.
   10. Give syntax and use of fwrite().
   - Ans. Refer to Section 8.3.
   11. Define union with example.
   - Ans. Refer to Section 6.4.
   12. Define macro with example.
   - Ans. Refer to Section 7.3.

2. **Attempt any four the following:**   [4 × 5 = 20]
   1. What are applications of 'C'?
   - Ans. Refer to Section 1.1.
   2. What is Dynamic memory allocation? Explain functions used to allocate and delete memory?
   - Ans. Refer to Section 4.9.
   3. Compare macro with functions.
   - Ans. Refer to Sections 4.1 and 7.3.
   4. Explain array of pointer to string with example.
   - Ans. Refer to Section 5.7.
   5. What is structure? Explain with example.
   - Ans. Refer to Section 6.1.

3. **Attempt any four of the following:** [4 × 5 = 20]
   1. Write a 'C' program to find maximum of three numbers.
Ans. Refer to Program 3.8 of Chapter 3.
   2. Write a 'C' program to check if given string in palindrome or not.
Ans. Refer to Program 5.28 of chapter 5.
   3. Write a 'C' program to count number of characters, number of words and number of lines from a text file and display result?
Ans. Refer to Programs in Chapter 8 and Program 4.42.
   4. Create a structure to store detail of 10 students as Roll No, name and percentage. Write a 'C' program to print Roll No, Names of students who have secured more than 70 percent.
Ans. Refer to Programs in Section 6.1.3.
   5. Write a 'C' program to accept a string from user and generate following pattern (e.g. input is string "abcd"):

   ```
   a
   a   b
   a   b   c
   a   b   c   d
   a   b   c
   a   b
   a
   ```

Ans. Refer to Programs to Chapter 3.

4. **Trace output and justify:** [5 × 4 = 20]

   1.
   ```
   Main()
   {
       union X
       {
           int a;
           float b;
           double c;
       }:
   printf("%\n", size of (x));
       a·x = 10;
   printf("%d%f%f/n", a.x, b.x, c.x)
       c.x = 1.23,
   printf("%d%f%f/n", a.x, b.x, c.x);
   }
   ```

Ans. **Output:**
Code shows errors as
Undefined symbol 'size', 'a', 'b', 'c'
Statement missing of line12
Function call missing) at line 9

2.
```
int test(int number)
{
    int m, n = 0;
    while (number)
    {
        m = number%10;
        if (m%2)
            n = n+1;
        number = number | 10;
    }
        return(n);
```
What will be the values of x and y when following statements are executed
```
        int x = test (135);
        int y = test (246);
```
Output:
```
values of x = 3
values of y = 0
```

3.
```
main()
{
    int a[5] = {5, 1, 15, 20, 25};
    int i, j, m;
    i = ++a[1];
    j = a[1]++;
    m=a[i++];
    printf(%d%d%d", i, j, m);
        getch();
}
```
Output: 3 2 15

4.
```
main()
{
    char *p = "a | qc";
    printf("%c...", ++ * (++p));
    printf("%c...", ++ p);
}
```
Output: m q

5. ```
   main()
   {
       state char str[ ] = "Malayalam",
       char *S;
       s = str + 8;
       while (s > = str)
       {
           printf("%c", *s);
           s--;
       }
   }
   ```
   Output: malayalaM
   ```